TEXT COPYRIGHT © [DR. PETER JOHNSON]

all rights reserved. No part of this guide may be reproduced in any form without permission in writing from the publisher except in the case of brief quotations embodied in critical articles or reviews.

Legal & disclaimer

The information contained in this book and its contents is not designed to replace or take the place of any form of medical or professional advice; and is not meant to replace the need for independent medical, financial, legal or other professional advice or services, as may be required. The content and information in this book have been provided for educational and entertainment purposes only.

The content and information contained in this book have been compiled from sources deemed reliable, and it is accurate to the best of the author's knowledge, information, and belief. However, the author cannot guarantee its accuracy and validity and cannot be held liable for any errors and/or omissions. Further, changes are periodically made to this book as and when needed. Where appropriate and/or necessary, you must consult a professional (including but not limited to your doctor, attorney, financial advisor or such other professional advisor) before using any of the suggested remedies, techniques, or information in this book.

Upon using the contents and information contained in this book, you agree to hold harmless the author from and against any damages, costs, and expenses, including any legal fees potentially resulting from the application of any of the information provided by this book. This disclaimer applies to any loss, damages or injury caused by the use and application, whether directly or indirectly, of any advice or information presented, whether for breach of contract, tort, negligence, personal injury, criminal intent, or under any other cause of action.

You agree to accept all risks of using the information presented inside this book.

You agree that by continuing to read this book, where appropriate and/or necessary, you shall consult a professional (including but not limited to your doctor, attorney, or financial advisor or such other advisor as needed) before using any of the suggested remedies, techniques, or information in this book.

Table of Contents

CIVIL LAW

Mastering Essential Legal Terms Explained About Civil Rights, Guardianship, Civil Transactions, Civil Obligations, Civil Liability, Civil Contracts And Civil Procedure!

DR. PETER JOHNSON

Copyright © 2019

All rights reserved.

ISBN: 9781798008102

Introduction

Thank you and congratulate you for downloading the book *"CIVIL LAW: Mastering Essential Legal Terms Explained About Civil Rights, Guardianship, Civil Transactions, Civil Obligations, Civil Liability, Civil Contracts and Civil Procedure!"*

With a clear, concise, and engaging writing style, Dr. Peter Johnson will help you with a practical understanding of civil law topics about civil rights, guardianship, civil transactions, security for performance of civil obligations, civil liability, civil contracts; provide you a road map to navigating civil procedure rules and help you build a foundation for understanding the overall picture and much much more. This book delivers extensive coverage of every aspect of the law and details the duties a paralegal is expected to perform when working within civil law and civil procedure. High-level, comprehensive coverage is combined with cutting-edge developments and foundational concepts.

As the author of the book, I promise this book will be an invaluable source of legal reference for professionals, international lawyers, law students, business professionals and anyone else who want to improve their use of legal terminology, succinct clarification of legal terms and have a better understanding of civil law and civil procedure. This book provides you with a comprehensive and highly practical approach in legal contexts, the world of civil law related to civil rights, guardianship, civil transactions, security for performance of civil obligations, civil liability, civil contracts, all substantive and procedural aspects of civil law. All legal terms and phrases are well written and explained clearly in plain English.

Thank you again for purchasing this book, and I hope you enjoy it.

Let's get started!

DEFINITION OF CIVIL LAW

Civil law is one part of the legal system regulating ordinary private matters. It includes different areas of law such as tort law, labor law, intellectual property law, and contract law. Civil law is also influenced by local traditions religious, practices, beliefs and culture.

BASIC PRINCIPLES OF CIVIL LAW

Principles of free and voluntary undertaking and agreement

The right to freely undertake or agree on the establishment of civil rights and obligations shall be guaranteed by law.

In civil relations, each person establishes, exercises/fulfills and terminates his/her civil rights and obligations on the basis of freely and voluntarily entering into commitments and/or agreements.

The principle of equality

In civil relations, each person shall be equal, may not use any reason for unequal treatment to others, and enjoy the same protection policies of law regarding moral rights and economic rights.

The principle of goodwill and honesty

In civil relations, each person must establish, exercise/ fulfill, or terminate his/her civil rights and/or obligations in the principle of goodwill and honesty.

The principle of bearing civil liability

The parties shall strictly perform their own civil obligations and shall be liable for his/her failure to fulfill or the incorrect fulfillment of any such civil obligations.

The principle of respect for good morals and traditions

The establishment, exercise and termination of civil rights and/or obligations may not infringe national interests, pubic interests, lawful rights and interests of other persons.

The principle of respect for, protection of, civil rights

1. All the civil rights of individuals, legal persons or other subjects shall be respected and protected by law.

2. When the civil rights of a subject are infringed upon, he/she/it shall have the right to protect such rights by him/her/itself in accordance with the provisions of law or request competent agencies or organizations to:

a/ Recognize his/her/its civil rights;

b/ Order the termination of the act of violation;

c/ Order a public apology and/or rectification;

d/ Order the performance of civil obligations;

e/ Order compensation for damage.

The principle of respect for State interests, public interests and legitimate rights and interests of other persons

The establishment and performance of civil rights and obligations must not infringe upon State interests, public interests and legitimate rights and interests of other persons.

The principle of compliance with law

The establishment and performance of civil rights and obligations must comply with the provisions of law.

The principle of conciliation

In civil relations, conciliation between the parties in accordance with the provisions of law shall be encouraged.

No one may use force or threaten to use force when participating in civil relations and/or resolving civil disputes.

ESTABLISHMENT AND EXERCISE OF CIVIL RIGHTS

Bases for establishment of civil rights

Civil rights shall be established on the following bases:

1. Contracts;

2. Unilateral legal acts;

3. Decisions of courts or other competent state agencies as prescribed;

4. Outcomes of labor, production and business; or creation of subjects of intellectual property rights;

5. Legitimate possession of property;

6. Illegal possession and use of assets or illegal gain therefrom;

7. Damage caused by an illegal act;

8. Performance of a task without authorization;

Exercise of civil rights

Each person shall exercise his/her civil on his/her own will in accordance with regulations of the Civil law.

INDIVIDUALS

CIVIL LEGAL CAPACITY, CIVIL ACT CAPACITY OF INDIVIDUALS

Civil legal capacity of individuals

1. The civil legal capacity of an individual is his/her capability to have civil rights and civil obligations.

2. All individuals shall have the same civil legal capacity.

3. The civil legal capacity of an individual shall exist from the time he/she is born and terminate when he/she dies.

Contents of the civil legal capacity of an individual

An individual shall have the following civil rights and obligations:

1. Personal rights not associated to property, and personal rights associated to property;

2. Ownership rights, inheritance rights and other rights with respect to property;

3. Rights to participate in civil relations and to assume obligations arising out of such relations.

The civil act capacity of an individual

The civil act capacity of an individual is his/her capability to establish and perform civil rights and obligations through his/her acts.

Adults and minors

Persons who are full eighteen years old or older are adults. Persons who are not yet full eighteen years old are minors.

Loss of civil act capacity

1. When a person is incapable of cognizing or controlling his/her acts due to mental disease or other ailments, the Court may, at the request of the person(s) with related rights or interests, issue a decision to declare such a person as having lost his/her civil act capacity, based on the conclusion of a competent medical examination body.

2. All civil transactions of persons who have lost their civil act capacity shall be established and performed by their representatives at law.

Restrictions on civil act capacity

1. Persons whose addiction to narcotics/drugs or to other stimulants leads to the squandering of their families' property may be declared by decision of the Court to be persons with a restricted civil act capacity, at the request of persons with related rights or interests or of relevant agencies or organizations.

2. Civil transactions related to the property of persons with a restricted civil act capacity must have the consents of their representatives at law, except for transactions to meet their daily-life needs.

PERSONAL RIGHTS

Personal rights

1. Personal rights are civil rights inherent to each natural person, which cannot be transferred to other persons.

2. All civil relations relating to personal rights of a minor or a legally incapacitated persons shall be established and performed with the consent of his/her legal representative.

The right with respect to family and given names

1. Each individual has the right to have a family name and a given name. The family and given names of a person shall be the family and given names in the birth certificate of such person.

The right to registration of birth

Individuals, when born, shall have the right to have their births registered.

The right to registration of death

When a person dies, his/her next of kin, the house owner or the agency or organization to which the dead person belonged must register the death of such person.

Right to nationality

1. Each individual has the right to nationality.

2. The identification, change, acquirement, renouncement, or assume of a particular nationality shall be stipulated in the Law on nationality of a particular country.

Rights of an individual with respect to his/her image

Each individual has rights with respect to his/her own image.

The use of an image of an individual must have his/her consent.

When an image of an individual is used for commercial purposes, that person is eligible for a remuneration, unless otherwise agreed.

Right to life, right to safety of life, health and body

1. Each individual has the right to life, the inviolable right to life and body, the right to health protection by law. No one shall be killed illegally.

2. When any person has a life-threatening accident or illness, a person who discovers such situation must take such person or require suitable entities to a nearest health facility; the health facility must provide medical examination and treatment in accordance with law on medical examination and treatment.

3. The consent of a person is required for the anesthesia, surgery, amputation, transplant of his/her tissues or bodily organs; the application of new medical cures to that person; medical, pharmacy or scientific testing or any method of testing on a human body.

If the person is a minor, a legally incapacitated person, a person with limited cognition or behavior control or an unconscious patient, the consent of his/her father, mother, spouse, grown child or legal guardian is required; in cases where there is a threat to the life of the patient which cannot wait for the consent of the aforesaid persons, a decision of the head of the health facility is required.

Right to protection of honor, dignity and prestige

1. Honor, dignity and prestige of an individual is inviolable and protected by law.

2. The person receiving the information adversely affected his/her honor, dignity and/or prestige both has the right to request rejection of such piece of information and has the right to require to informing person gives a public apology and rectification and compensation.

The right to donation of body organs

Individuals shall have the right to donate their body organs for the purpose of medical treatment of other persons or scientific research.

The donation and use of body organs shall comply with the provisions of law.

The right to donation of corpses, body organs after death

Individuals shall have the right to donate their corpses, body organs after they die for the purpose of medical treatment of other persons or scientific research.

The donation and use of corpses, body organs of dead persons shall comply with the provisions of law.

The right to receive body organs

Individuals shall have the right to receive body organs of other persons for their medical treatment.

It is strictly forbidden to receive and use body organs of other persons for commercial purposes.

The right to re-determination of gender

Individuals shall have the right to the re-determination of their gender.

The re-determination of gender of a person shall be performed in cases where his/her gender is affected with inborn defects or has not been properly shaped, which needs the medical intervention to clearly determine the gender.

The re-determination of gender shall comply with the provisions of law.

The right to personal secrets

1. The private life, personal secrets and family secrets of a person are inviolable and protected by law.

2. The collection, preservation, use and publication of information about the private life of an individual must have the consent of that person; the collection, preservation, use and publication of information about the secrets of family must have the consent of all family's members, unless otherwise prescribed by law.

3. The safety of mails, telephones, telegrams, other forms of electronic information of an individual shall be ensured and kept confidential.

The opening, control and keeping of mails, telephones, telegrams, other forms of electronic information of an individual may only be conducted in cases provided by law.

4. Contracting parties of a contract may not disclose information about each other's private life, personal secrets or family secrets that they know during the establishment and performance of the contract, unless otherwise agreed.

The right to marriage

Males and females who have fully met the conditions for marriage in accordance with the law on marriage and family shall have the right to marriage at their free will.

The right to equality between husband and wife

Husband and wife are equal to each other, shall have the same rights and obligations in all respects in family and in civil relations and shall together build a plentiful, equitable, progressive, happy and lasting family.

The right to enjoy mutual care among family members

The members of a family shall have the right to enjoy mutual care and assistance.

Children and grandchildren who are minors shall benefit from the care and upbringing of the mother, father and grandparents; children and grand-children shall have the duty to respect, care for and support their parents and grandparents.

The right to divorce

A wife or husband or both the wife and the husband shall have the right to request the Court to solve their divorce.

The right to recognize or not to recognize a father, mother or child

1. A person who is not recognized as a father, mother or child of another person shall have the right to request a competent state agency to determine him/her as father, mother or child of that person.

2. A person who is recognized as a father, mother or child of another person shall have the right to request a competent state agency to determine him/her as not being father, mother or child of that person.

The right to adopt a child and the right to be accepted as an adoptive child

An individual's right to adopt a child and right to be accepted as an adoptive child shall be recognized and protected by law.

The adoption of a child and the process of being accepted as an adoptive child shall comply with the provisions of law.

The inviolable right to place of residence

Individuals shall have the inviolable right to their places of residence.

The entry into the place of residence of a person must be consented by that person.

The search of a place of residence of a person shall be performed only in cases where it is so provided for by law and where there is a warrant from a competent state agency; the search must comply with the order and procedures specified by law.

The right to freedom of belief and religion

1. Individuals shall have the right to freedom of belief and religion, and to adhere to or not to adhere to a religion.

2. No one may infringe upon the freedom of belief and religion, or abuse beliefs or religions to infringe upon State interests, public interests or legitimate rights and interests of other persons.

The right to freedom of movement, freedom of residence

1. Individuals shall have the right to freedom of travel and freedom of residence.

2. An individual's freedom of travel and/or freedom of residence may be restricted only by decision of a competent state agency and in accordance with the order and procedures specified by law.

The right to work

Individuals shall have the right to work.

Every person shall have the right to work, the freedom to choose a job or occupation without being discriminated against on the ground of his/her ethnicity, sex, social status, belief or religion.

The right to freedom of business

Individuals' right to freedom of business shall be respected and protected by law.

Individuals shall have the right to choose the forms, areas and lines of business, to establish enterprises, to freely enter into contracts and hire labor, and other rights in accordance with the provisions of law.

PLACE OF RESIDENCE

Place of residence of individuals

The place of residence of an individual is the place where such person usually lives.

Place of residence of minors

The place of residence of a minor is the place of residence of his/her parents; if the parents have separate places of residence, the place of residence of the minor shall be the place of residence of the father or mother with whom the minor usually lives.

GUARDIANSHIP

Guardianship

Guardianship means an individual or organization (hereinafter referred collectively to as guardian) is required by law or appointed to take care of and protect legitimate rights and interests of a minor or a legally incapacitated person or a person with limited cognition and behavior control (hereinafter referred to as a ward).

Wards

Wards include:

a) Minors who have lost their mothers and fathers, or whose parents are unidentifiable;

b) Minors whose parents are both incapacitated persons; parents have limited cognition or behavior control; parents have limited capacity of exercise; parents have their parental rights restricted by a court; and parents do not have the means to care for or educate such minor and the parents request the minor to be a ward;

c) Incapacitated persons;

d) Persons with limited cognition or behavior control.

Guardians

Each natural person or legal person who meets all requirements prescribed by law will be entitled to be a guardian.

Requirements for natural persons to be guardians

Each natural person who meets all of the following requirements may act as a guardian:

1. Having full legal capacity;

2. Having good ethics and necessary means to exercise rights and fulfill obligations of a guardian;

3. Not being a person facing a criminal prosecution or a person who has been convicted but his/her criminal record has been not expunged for a deliberate crime of violation of life, health, honor, dignity or property of another person;

Obligations of guardians

The guardian of a person shall have the following obligations:

1. To educate and take care of the ward.

2. To represent the ward in civil transactions,

3. To manage the property of the ward.

4. To protect legitimate rights and interests of the ward.

Rights of guardians

The guardian of a minor or a legally incapacitated person shall have the following rights:

a) Use the property of the ward in order to take care of and pay for the needs of the ward;

b) Receive payment of all necessary expenditures on management of the property of the ward;

c) Represent the ward in the establishment and performance of civil transactions in order to protect legitimate rights and interests of the ward.

Termination of guardianship

A guardianship shall be terminated in any of the following cases:

a) The ward attains full legal capacity;

b) The ward dies;

c) The ward's father and/or mother have/has fully met the conditions to exercise his/her rights or fulfill his/her obligations;

d) The ward has been adopted.

LEGAL PERSONS

Legal persons

An organization shall be recognized as a legal person when it meets all the following conditions:

a) It is legally established.

b) It has a well-organized structure;

c) It has property independent from other individuals and other organizations, and bears liability by recourse to its property;

d) It participates independently in legal relations in its own name.

Establishment of legal persons

A legal person may be established on the initiative of an individual or an organization, or under a decision of a competent state agency.

The civil legal capacity of legal persons

1. The civil legal capacity of a legal person is its capability to have civil rights and obligations consistent with the purpose of its operation.

2. The civil legal capacity of a legal person shall arise from the time it is established and shall terminate from the time it ceases to be a legal person.

3. The representative at law or the authorized representative of a legal person shall act in the name of the legal person in civil relations.

The name of a legal person

1. A legal person must have its own name which shall clearly indicate the legal person's organizational form and distinguish it from other legal persons operating in the same domain.

2. A legal person must use its own name in civil transactions.

3. The name of a legal person shall be recognized and protected by law.

Consolidation of legal persons

1. Legal persons may consolidate into a new legal person.

2. After consolidation, the former legal persons shall cease to exist from the time of establishment of the new legal person; the civil rights and obligations of the former legal persons shall be transferred to the new legal person.

Acquisition of legal persons

1. A legal person (hereinafter referred to as acquired legal person) may be merged into another legal person (hereinafter referred to as acquiring legal person).

2. After acquisition, the acquired legal person shall cease to exist; the civil rights and obligations of the acquired legal person shall be transferred to the acquiring legal person.

Division of legal persons

1. A legal person may be divided into many legal persons under the provisions of its charter or the decision of a competent state agency.

2. After division, the divided legal person shall terminate; the civil rights and obligations of such legal person shall be transferred to the new legal persons.

Total division of legal persons

1. A legal person may be totally divided to multiple legal persons.

2. After total division, the transferor legal person shall cease to exist; the civil rights and obligations of the transferor legal person shall be transferred to new legal persons.

Partial division of legal persons

1. A legal person may be partially divided to multiple legal persons.

2. After partial division, the transferor legal person and transferee legal persons shall perform their civil rights and obligations in accordance with their own operation objectives.

Conversion of forms of legal persons

1. The form of a legal person may be converted into another form.

2. After conversion of form, the converting legal person shall cease to exist from the time of establishment of the converted legal person, the civil rights and obligations of the converting legal person shall be transferred to the converted legal person.

Dissolution of legal persons

1. A legal person shall be dissolved in any of the following cases:

a) In accordance with the provisions of its charter;

b) Pursuant to a decision of a competent authority;

c) Upon expiry of its term of operation as provided in its charter or in the decision of the competent authority;

2. Prior to dissolution, a legal person must fulfill all of its property obligations.

Termination of legal persons

1. A legal person shall terminate in any of the following cases:

a) Consolidation, acquisition, total division, conversion of legal person, or dissolution;

b) Declaration of bankruptcy in accordance with law on bankruptcy.

2. A legal person shall terminate from the time its name is removed from the legal person registry or as from the time stated in a decision of competent authority.

3. When a legal person terminates, its property shall be resolved in accordance with provisions of law.

TYPES OF LEGAL PERSON

Commercial legal persons

1. Commercial legal person means a legal person whose primary purpose is seeking profits and its profits shall be distributed to its members.

2. Commercial legal persons include enterprises and other business entities.

Non-commercial legal persons

1. Non-commercial legal person means a legal person whose primary purpose is not seeking profits and its possible profits may not distributed to its members.

2. Commercial legal persons include regulatory agencies, people's armed units, political organizations, socio-political organizations, political-socio-professional organizations, social organizations, socio-professional organizations, social funds, charitable funds, social enterprises and other non-commercial organizations.

CIVIL TRANSACTIONS

Civil transactions

Civil transaction is a contract or a unilateral legal act which gives rise to, changes or terminates civil rights and/or obligations.

Conditions for effective civil transactions

A civil transaction shall be effective when it satisfies all of the following conditions:

a) Participants in the transaction have legal personality and/or legal capacity in conformity with such transaction;

b) Participants in the civil transaction act completely voluntarily;

c) The purpose and contents of the transaction are not contrary to the law.

Objectives of civil transactions

The objectives of civil transactions are legitimate interests which the parties wish to obtain when establishing such transactions.

Forms of civil transactions

A civil transaction shall be expressed verbally or in writing, or through specific acts.

Interpretation of civil transactions

In cases where a civil transaction may be understood in different ways, such transaction must be interpreted in the following order:

a/ According to the true aspirations of the parties when the transaction is established;

b/ According to the meaning consistent with the objective of the transaction;

c/ According to the practices of the locality where the transaction is established.

INVALID CIVIL TRANSACTIONS

Invalidity of civil transactions due to breach of legal prohibitions or contravention of social ethics

Civil transactions with purposes and contents violating prohibitory provisions of law or contravening social ethics shall be invalid.

Prohibitory provisions of law mean the provisions of law which do not permit subjects to perform certain acts.

Social ethics are common standards of conduct among people in social life, which are recognized and respected by the community.

Invalidity of civil transactions due to falsity

When the parties falsely establish a civil transaction in order to conceal another transaction, the false transaction shall be invalid and the concealed transaction remains valid.

Invalidity of civil transactions established and performed by minors or legally incapacitated persons or persons with limited legal capacity

When a civil transaction is established or performed by a minor, a legally incapacitated person, or a person with limited legal capacity, a court shall, at the request of the representative of that person, declare such transaction invalid, if it is provided for by law that such transaction must be established and performed by or with the consent of the representative of that person,

Invalidity of civil transactions due to misunderstanding

When a party has established a transaction due to its misunderstanding of the contents of the transaction due to unintentional mistakes made by the other party, it shall have the right to request the other party to change the contents of such transaction; if the other party does not accept such request, the mistaken party shall have the right to request the Court to declare the transaction invalid.

Invalidity of civil transactions due to deception, threat or compulsion

Any party entering into a civil transaction as a result of deception, threat or compulsion has the right to request a court to declare such transaction invalid.

Deception in a civil transaction means an intentional act of a party or a third person, aiming to induce the other party to misunderstand the subject, the nature of the object or the content of the civil transaction and thus to agree to enter into such transaction.

Threat or compulsion in a civil transaction means an intentional act of a party or a third person which compels the other party to conduct the civil transaction in order to avoid danger to the life, health, honor, reputation, dignity and/or property or that of its relatives.

Invalidity of civil transactions due to establishment by persons incapable of being aware of and controlling their acts

A person who has the civil act capacity but established a civil transaction at a time he/she was incapable of being aware of and controlling his/her acts shall have the right to request the Court to declare such civil transaction invalid.

Partially invalid civil transactions

A civil transaction shall be partially invalid when one part of the transaction is invalid, provided that such part does not affect the validity of the remaining parts of the transaction.

Legal consequences of invalid civil transactions

1. An invalid civil transaction shall not give rise to, change or terminate any civil rights and obligations of the parties as from the time the transaction is entered into.

2. When a civil transaction is invalid, the parties shall be restored to the original status and shall return to each other what they have received; if the return cannot be made in kind, it shall be made in money. The party at fault, which caused damage, must compensate therefore.

REPRESENTATION

Representation

Representation is the act of a person (hereinafter referred to as the representative) to establish and perform a civil transaction in the name and interests of another person (hereinafter referred to as the represented person) within the scope of representation.

Basis for establishment of representation rights

Representation rights shall be established according to a power of attorney between a principal and a representative (hereinafter referred to as authorized representation); according to a decision of a competent authority, a charter of a legal person or as prescribed by law (hereinafter referred to as legal representation).

Representatives at law

Representatives at law shall include:

1. Fathers and/or mothers with respect to children who are minors;

2. Guardians with respect to wards;

3. Heads of family households with respect to family households;

4. Heads of cooperative groups with respect to cooperative groups;

Representation under authorization

Representation under authorization is the representation established under an authorization between the representative and the represented person.

Representatives under authorization

Individuals, representatives at law of legal persons may authorize other persons to establish and/or perform civil transactions.

Termination of representation of individuals

1. The representation at law of an individual shall terminate in the following cases:

a/ The represented person has attained adulthood or has had his/her civil act capacity restored;

b/ The represented person dies;

2. The representation under authorization of individuals shall terminate in the following cases:

a/ The authorization time limit has expired or the authorized work has been completed;

b/ The authorizing persons revoke the authorization, or the authorized persons refuse the authorization;

c/ The authorizing persons or the authorized persons die, have been declared by the Court as having lost their civil act capacity, having their civil act capacity restricted, having been missing or dead.

Upon the termination of the authorized representation, the representatives must fulfill the property obligations towards the represented persons or the heirs of the represented persons.

Termination of representation of legal persons

1. The representation at law of legal persons shall terminate when such legal persons cease to exist.

2. The representation under authorization of legal persons shall terminate in the following cases:

a/ The authorization time limit has expired or the authorized work has been completed;

b/ The representatives at law of the legal persons revoke the authorization or the authorized persons refuse the authorization;

c/ The legal persons cease to exist or the authorized persons die, have been declared by the Court as having lost their civil act capacity, having their civil act capacity restricted, having been missing or dead.

Upon the termination of representation under authorization, the representatives must fulfill the property obligations towards the authorizing legal persons or inheriting legal persons.

STATUTE OF LIMITATIONS

Statute of limitations

A statute of limitations is a time limit specified by law upon the expiration of which a subject may enjoy civil rights, be released from civil obligations or lose the right to initiate a civil lawsuit or the right to request the settlement of civil matters.

Method of calculating a statute of limitations

A statute of limitations shall be calculated from the point of time which begins the first day of the statute of limitations and shall end at the point of time which ends the last day of the statute of limitations.

PROPERTY

Property

1. Property comprises tangible things, money, valuable papers and property rights.

2. Property includes immovable property and movable property. Immovable property and movable property may be existing property or off-plan property.

Immovable property and movable property

1. Immovable property includes:

a) Land;

b) Houses and constructions attached to land;

c) Other property attached to land, houses and constructions;

2. Moveable property is property which is not immovable property.

Yield and income

1. Yields are natural products which property generates.

2. Profits are incomes derived from the exploitation of property.

Property rights

Property rights are rights which are able to be valued in money, including property rights to subjects of intellectual property rights, right to use land and other property rights.

OWNERSHIP RIGHTS

Ownership rights

Ownership rights comprise the rights of an owner to possession, to use and to disposition of his/her property.

Owners are individuals, legal persons or other subjects, having all three rights which are the right to possession, the right to use and the right to disposition of their property.

Protection of ownership rights.

1. Ownership rights of individuals, legal persons or other subjects shall be recognized and protected by law.

2. No one may be illegally restricted in or deprived of his/her ownership rights to his/her property.

Measures for protection of ownership rights

Each owner is entitled to self-protect and prevent anyone from infringing his/her rights by requesting a court or another competent authority to compel the person infringing upon their rights to return the property and terminate the acts of illegally obstructing the exercise of their ownership rights, and to request compensation for any damage.

The right to reclaim property

Owners and/or holders of other property-related rights shall have the right to request the persons possessing, using or receiving benefits from the property without a legal basis to return such property.

The right to request compensation for damage

Owners are entitled to request persons infringing upon their ownership rights to compensate for any damage.

Bases for establishing ownership rights

Ownership rights to property shall be established in the following cases:

1. Through labor or lawful production and business activities;

2. Ownership rights are transferred under an agreement or a decision of a competent state agency;

3. Yields and profits gained;

4. A new thing created from merger, mixture or processing;

5. Inheritance of property;

Bases for termination of ownership rights

Ownership rights shall terminate in the following cases:

1. The owner transfers his/her ownership rights to another person;

2. The owner renounces his/her ownership rights;

3. The property is destroyed;

4. The property is disposed of for the discharge of the owner's obligations;

5. The property is compulsorily purchased;

6. The property is confiscated;

CONTENTS OF OWNERSHIP RIGHTS

THE RIGHT TO POSSESSION

The right to possession

The right to possession is the right to keep and manage a property directly or indirectly as holder of rights to such property.

Possession with a legal basis

Possession with a legal basis is the possession of a property in the following cases:

1. The owner possesses the property;

2. A person is authorized by the owner to manage the property;

3. A person to whom the right to possession has been transferred through a civil transaction in accordance with the provisions of law;

Possession without legal bases

Possession without legal bases means that the possession that the possessor knew or should have known that he/she has no right to the property under his/her possession.

THE RIGHT TO USE

The right to use

The right to use means the right to exploit the utility of, and to enjoy the yields and profits from, the property.

The right to use of owners

The owner has the right to use property in conformity with his/her wishes provided that this will not cause damage to or adversely affect the interests of the State or the public or the legal rights and interests of other persons.

THE RIGHT TO DISPOSITION

The right to disposition

The right to disposition means the right to transfer property ownership rights, renounce ownership rights, right to use, or destruct the property.

Conditions for disposition

The disposition of property must be performed by persons having the civil act capacity in accordance with the provisions of law.

Owner's right to disposition

Owners shall have the right to sell, exchange, donate, lend, bequeath, abandon or dispose of their property in accordance with the provisions of law.

FORMS OF OWNERSHIP

THE PEOPLE'S OWNERSHIP

Property under the people's ownership

Land, water resources, mineral resources, resources in the waters, airspace and other natural resources and the assets invested and/or managed by the State belong to the entire people with the representation and centralized management of the State.

COLLECTIVE OWNERSHIP

Collective ownership

Collective ownership means ownership by cooperatives or other stable economic entities in which individuals and/or households jointly contribute capital and labor for production and business cooperation to achieve common goals stated in their charters and on the principles of voluntariness, equality, democracy and joint management and mutual benefit.

Property under collective ownership

Property constituted from the contributions of members, legitimate income from production and business, supports from the State or other sources that accord with the provisions of law shall be property under the ownership of such collectives.

Possession, use and disposition of property under collective ownership

1. The possession, use and disposition of property under collective ownership must comply with law, accord with the charters of the collectives and ensure the stable development of collective ownership.

2. Property under collective ownership may be assigned to members for exploitation of the utility thereof by their labor in production and business activities in order to serve the common need for production expansion and economic development as well as the interests and needs of the members.

3. The members of a collective shall have the pre-emptive right to purchase, lease or package- lease property under collective ownership.

PRIVATE OWNERSHIP

Private ownership

Private ownership means ownership of individuals over their lawful property.

Private ownership comprises personal ownership by individuals, ownership by small business owners and private capitalist ownership.

Property under private ownership

Legitimate income, savings, residential houses, means of daily life, means of production, capital, yields and profits and other lawful properties of an individual constitute property under private ownership.

Lawful property under private ownership shall not be limited in quantity and value.

Possession, use and disposition of property under private ownership

1. Individuals shall have the right to possession, use and disposition of property under their respective ownership to meet the needs of daily life, consumption or production and business and other purposes in accordance with the provisions of law.

2. The possession, use and disposition of property under private ownership must not cause damage to or affect State interests, public interests or legitimate rights and interests of other persons.

COMMON OWNERSHIP

Common ownership

Common ownership means ownership of property by more than one owner.

Common ownership comprises common ownership by shares and common ownership by integration.

A property under common ownership is a common property.

Establishment of common ownership right

A common ownership right is established under the agreement of the owners, under the provisions of law or in accordance with practices.

Common ownership by shares

1. Common ownership by shares means common ownership in which each owner's share of the ownership right to the common property is determined.

2. Each of the owners of property under common ownership by shares shall have his/her rights and obligations to such property corresponding to his/her share of the ownership right, unless otherwise agreed upon.

Common ownership by integration

1. Common ownership by integration means common ownership in which each owner's share of the ownership right to the common property is not determined.

Common ownership by integration comprises divisible common ownership by integration and indivisible common ownership by integration.

2. Owners of property under common ownership by integration shall have equal rights and obligations to the property under common ownership.

Common ownership by husband and wife

1. Common ownership by husband and wife is common ownership by integration.

2. Husband and wife who jointly establish and develop the common property through the efforts of each shall have equal rights in the possession, use and disposition of such property.

3. Husband and wife shall discuss, agree or authorize each other to the possession, use and disposition of the common property.

4. The common property of husband and wife may be divided by their agreement or by a decision of the Court.

Possession of common property

Owners of property under common ownership shall jointly manage the common property according to the principle of unanimity.

Use of common property

1. Each owner of property under common ownership by shares shall have the right to exploit the utility of, and enjoy the yields and profits from, the common property corresponding to his/her share in the ownership right, unless otherwise agreed upon.

2. Owners of property under common ownership by integration shall have equal rights to exploit the utility of, and enjoy the yields and profits from, the common property, unless otherwise agreed upon.

Disposition of common property

1. Each owner of property under common ownership by shares shall have the right to dispose of his/her own share in the ownership right as agreed upon.

2. The disposition of property under common ownership by integration shall be performed in accordance with the agreement of the co-owners.

Termination of common ownership

A common ownership shall terminate in the following cases:

1. The common property has been divided;

2. One of the co-owners is entitled to the entire common property;

3. The common property no longer exists;

CIVIL OBLIGATIONS

Civil obligations

Civil obligations mean acts whereby one or more entities (hereinafter referred to as obligors) must transfer objects, transfer rights, pay money or provide valuable papers, perform other acts or refrain from performing certain acts in the interests of one or more other subjects (hereinafter referred to as obligees).

Bases for giving rise to obligations

A civil obligation shall arise on the following bases:

1. A civil contract;

2. A unilateral legal act;

3. Performance of a task without authorization;

4. Possession and use of property or enjoyment of benefits from property without a legal basis;

5. Causing damage by performing an illegal act;

6. Performance of a task without authorization;

Objects of civil obligations

1. An object of a civil obligation may be a property or a task which must or must not be performed.

2. An object of a civil obligation must be specifically determined.

PERFORMANCE OF CIVIL OBLIGATIONS

The principle for performance of civil obligations

An obligor must perform his/her obligation in an honest manner, in the spirit of cooperation, in a manner faithful to his/her commitment and not contrary to law.

Time limit for performance of civil obligations

1. The time limit for performing a civil obligation shall be agreed upon by the parties.

The obligor must perform his/her civil obligation on time; may perform the civil obligation before the specified time limit only if the obligee so consents; if the obligor has performed the obligation before the specified time limit at his/her own will and the obligee has accepted such performance, the obligation shall be considered to have been performed on time.

2. In cases where the time limit for the performance of a civil obligation has not been agreed upon by the parties or specified by the law, the parties may perform the obligation or request the performance of the obligation at any time, but must notify each other in advance within a reasonable period of time.

Delay in performance of civil obligations

1. The delay in performance of a civil obligation means the obligation has not been performed yet or has been partially performed upon the expiration of the time limit for performance of the obligation.

2. The party that delays the performance of a civil obligation must immediately notify the obligee of the non-performance of the obligation on time.

Postponement of performance of civil obligations

1. When it is impossible to fulfill a civil obligation on time, the obligor must immediately inform the obligee thereof and propose the postponement of the performance of the obligation.

In case of failure to inform the obligee, the obligor must compensate for the arising damage, except in cases where it is otherwise agreed upon or the notification cannot be made due to objective causes.

2. The obligor may postpone the performance of an obligation if the obligee so agrees. The postponed performance of a civil obligation shall still be considered a timely performance.

Delay in acceptance of performance of civil obligations

1. The delay in acceptance of the performance of a civil obligation means that, upon the expiration of the time limit for the fulfillment of the civil obligation, the obligor has already fulfilled the civil obligation as agreed upon, but the obligee does not accept the performance of such obligation.

2. In case of delay in accepting the civil obligation's object being a property, the obligor must take necessary measures to preserve the property and shall be entitled to request the reimbursement of reasonable expenses.

3. With respect to a property which is in imminent danger of decay, the obligor shall have the right to sell such property and return the proceeds from the sale of such property to the obligee after deducting necessary expenses for the preservation and sale of such property.

CIVIL LIABILITY

Civil liability for breach of civil obligations

1. An obligor that fails to perform or performs improperly his/her/its obligation must bear civil liability to the obligee.

Breach of obligations means that the obligor fails to perform the obligations on time, perform the obligations incompletely or incorrectly.

2. In cases where an obligor is not able to perform a civil obligation due to a force majeure event, he/she/it shall not have to bear any civil liability, unless otherwise agreed upon or provided for by law.

3. The obligor shall not have to bear civil liability if he/she/it can prove that the failure to perform the obligation is due entirely to the fault of the obligee.

Liability to compensate for damage

1. The liability to compensate for damage includes the liability to compensate for material damage and the liability to compensate for mental damage.

2. The liability to compensate for material damage is the liability to make up for the actual material losses caused by the breaching party, which can be calculated in money and include the loss of property, reasonable expenses incurred in preventing, mitigating and/or redressing the damage and the actual loss or reduction of income.

3. A person causing mental damage to another person by infringing upon the life, health, honor, dignity or prestige of such person shall have to pay pecuniary compensation to the victim in addition to stopping the infringement, offering an apology and making public rectification.

Late performance of civil obligations

1. Late performance of a civil obligation is the failure to have performed the civil obligation in whole or in part as at the expiry of the time-limit for the performance of such obligation.

2. The party being late in performance of a civil obligation must notify immediately the obligee about the failure to have performed the civil obligation in a timely manner.

Postponement of performance of civil obligations

1. When it is not possible to perform a civil obligation on time, the obligor must inform immediately the obligee and may suggest postponement of performance of the civil obligation.

In the case of failure to notify the obligee, the obligor must compensate for any damage arising, unless otherwise agreed or unless it was impossible to provide notification due to objective reasons.

2. The obligor may postpone the performance of the obligation only if the obligee consents. The performance of the civil obligation in this case of postponement shall be deemed to be performance in a timely manner.

Late acceptance of performance of civil obligations

1. The late acceptance of the performance of a civil obligation is where the time-limit for the fulfillment of the civil obligation has expired and the obligor has already fulfilled the civil obligation as agreed but the obligee does not accept the performance of such obligation.

Liability for late performance of the obligation to pay

Where the obligor makes late payment, then it must pay interest on the unpaid amount corresponding to the late period.

Liability for late acceptance of performance of civil obligations

An obligee which is late in accepting the performance of a civil obligation, and thereby causes damage to the obligor, must compensate the obligor for any damage and shall accept all risks arising from the time when acceptance fell due, unless otherwise agreed.

Liability for compensation due to breach of obligations

With respect to damage caused by breach of an obligation, the obligor must compensate for the whole damage, unless otherwise agreed or prescribed by law.

Damage caused by breach of obligations

1. Damage caused by breach of obligations comprises physical damage and spiritual damage.

2. The physical damage means those actual physical losses, comprising loss of property, reasonable expenses to prevent, mitigate or restore damage, and the actual loss or reduction of income.

3. Spiritual damage means losses related to life, health, honor, dignity or reputation and other personal benefits of an entity.

The obligation to prevent or limit damage

The obligee must adopt the necessary and reasonable measures to prevent or limit its damage.

Compensation for damages in case of the aggrieved party at fault

Where the breach of the obligations and damage incurred due to part of the fault of the aggrieved party, the violating party only be required to pay damages corresponding to its degree of fault.

Fault in civil liability

Fault in civil liability includes intentional fault and unintentional fault.

Intentional fault means that a person is fully aware that its act will cause damage to another person but, nevertheless, performs the act and, irrespective of whether or not it so wishes, allows the damage to occur.

Unintentional means that a person does not foresee that its act is capable of causing damage, even though it knows or should know that the damage will occur, or where it does foresee that such act is capable of causing damage but believes that the damage will not occur or will be able to be prevented.

SECURITY FOR PERFORMANCE OF OBLIGATIONS

Types of security for performance of obligations

Types of security for the performance of obligations comprise the following:

a/ Pledge of property;

b/ Mortgage of property;

c/ Deposit;

d/ Security collateral;

e/ Escrow account;

f/ Guaranty;

g/ Pledge of trust.

Objects used to secure the performance of civil obligations

1. Objects used to secure the performance of civil obligations must be under the ownership rights of the securing party and be permitted for transaction.

2. Objects used to secure the performance of civil obligations are the existing objects or objects to be formed in the future. Objects to be formed in the future are movable property or immovable property under the ownership of the securing party after the time the obligations are established or the security transactions are entered into.

Property rights used to secure the performance of civil obligations

1. Property rights owned by the securing party, including property rights arising from copyrights, industrial property rights, rights to plant varieties, the right to claim debts, the right to receive insurance indemnities for secured objects, property rights to capital amounts contributed to enterprises, property rights arising from contracts and other property rights of the securing party, may all be used to secure the performance of civil obligations.

2. Land use rights may be used to secure the performance of civil obligations.

PLEDGE OF PROPERTY

Pledge of property

The pledge of a property is a transaction in which a party (hereinafter referred to as the pledgor) hands over a property to the other party (hereinafter referred to as the pledgee) to secure the performance of a civil obligation(s).

Forms of pledge of property

The pledge of property must be established in writing, either in a separate document or incorporated in a principal contract.

Effect of pledge of property

A pledge of property shall take effect as from the time of handing over the property to the pledgee.

Duration of pledge of property

The duration of a pledge of property shall be agreed upon by the parties.

Obligations of the property pledgor

The property pledgor shall have the following obligations:

1. To hand over the pledged property to the pledgee as agreed upon;

2. To notify the pledgee of the right of a third party to the pledged property, if any; in the absence of such notification, the pledgee shall have the right to cancel the property pledge contract and demand compensation for damage, or to maintain the contract and accept the rights of the third party to the pledged property;

3. To pay the pledgee reasonable expenses incurred for maintaining and preserving the pledged property, unless otherwise agreed upon.

Rights of the property pledgor

1. Require the pledgee to suspend use of the pledged property if the pledged property is in danger of losing its value or depreciating in value as a result of such use.

2. Require the pledgee to hold the pledged property to return the pledged property and related documents after the obligation secured by the pledge has been fulfilled.

3. Require the pledgee to compensate for any damage caused to the pledged property.

4. Sell, substitute, exchange, or give the pledged property to other property if so agreed by the pledgee or prescribed by law.

Obligations of the property pledgee

The property pledgee shall have the following obligations:

1. To maintain and preserve the pledged property; if causing loss of, or damage to, the pledged property, to pay compensation for damage to the pledgor;

2. Not to sell, exchange, donate, lease, or lend the pledged property; not to use the pledged property to secure the performance of another obligation;

3. Not to exploit the utility of, or enjoy the yields and/or profits from, the pledged property, if not so consented by the pledgor;

4. To return the pledged property upon the termination of the obligation which is secured by the pledge or when it is replaced by another security measure.

Rights of the property pledgee

The property pledgee shall have the following rights:

1. To demand that the person unlawfully possessing or using the pledged property return the property;

2. To demand that the pledged property be disposed of in the manner as agreed upon or provided for by law for the performance of an obligation;

3. To exploit the utility of, and enjoy the yields and/or profits from, the pledged property, if so agreed upon;

4. To be paid reasonable expenses for the preservation of the pledged property when returning the pledged property to the pledgor.

Termination of pledges on property

The pledge of property shall terminate in the following cases:

1. The obligation secured by the pledge has terminated;

2. The pledge of property has been cancelled or substituted by another security measure;

3. The pledged property has been disposed of;

4. It is so agreed by the parties.

MORTGAGES ON PROPERTY

Mortgage of property

1. The mortgage of property means the use by a party (hereinafter referred to as the mortgagor) of his/her/its own property to secure the performance of a civil obligation toward the other party (hereinafter referred to as the mortgagee) without transferring such property to the mortgagee.

In cases where an entire immovable or movable property containing an auxiliary object is mortgaged, the auxiliary object of such immovable or immovable property shall also belong to the mortgaged property.

In cases where only part of the immovable or movable property containing an auxiliary object is mortgaged, the auxiliary object shall belong to the mortgaged property, unless otherwise agreed upon by the parties.

The mortgaged property can also be the property to be formed in the future.

2. The mortgaged property shall be held by the mortgagor. The parties may agree to let a third party keep the mortgaged property.

Forms of property mortgage

The mortgage of property must be made in writing, either in a separate document or incorporated in a principal contract.

Duration of mortgage

The parties shall agree on the duration of a mortgage of property; in the absence of such agreement, the mortgage shall last until the termination of the obligation secured by the mortgage.

Obligations of the property mortgagor

The property mortgagor shall have the following obligations:

1. Transfer documents related to the mortgaged property, unless otherwise agreed.

2. Take care of and preserve the mortgaged property.

3. If the mortgaged property is in danger of losing its value or depreciating in value due to its exploitation, to take necessary remedial measures, including ceasing the exploitation of the mortgaged property.

4. When the mortgaged property is damaged, the mortgagor is obligated to, within a reasonable period, repair or substitute another property with equivalent value, unless otherwise agreed.

5. Provide information about the actual condition of the mortgaged property to for the mortgagee.

6. Notify the mortgagee of any third person rights with respect to the mortgaged property (if any). In the case of failure to provide such notice, the mortgagee shall have the right to cancel the contract of mortgage of property and demand compensation for damage or the right to maintain the contract and agree on the rights of the third person with respect to the mortgaged property.

7. Do not sell, exchange or give the mortgaged property.

Rights of the property mortgagor

The property mortgagor shall have the following rights:

1. To exploit the utility of, and enjoy the yields and profits from, the property, except in cases where the yields and profits also belong to the mortgaged property as agreed upon;

2. To invest so as to increase the value of the mortgaged property;

3. To sell, replace the mortgaged property if such property is a commodity circulated in the process of production and/or business;

4. To sell, exchange or donate the mortgaged property other than a commodity circulated in the process of production and/or business, if so agreed by the mortgagee;

5. To lease, lend the mortgaged property but with the notification to the lessee or the borrower that the leased or lent property is being mortgaged, and to have to notify such to the mortgagee;

6. To reclaim the mortgaged property held by a third party, when the obligation secured by the mortgage is terminated or secured by another measure.

Obligations of the property mortgagee

The property mortgagee shall return to the mortgagor the papers on the mortgaged property upon termination of the mortgage in cases where the parties agree that the mortgagee keeps the papers on the mortgaged property;

Rights of the property mortgagee

The property mortgagee shall have the following rights:

1. To demand that the lessee or the borrower of the mortgaged property terminate the use of the mortgaged property, if such use causes the loss or decrease of the value of such property;

2. To directly check and inspect the mortgaged property but not to hinder or cause difficulty to the use or exploitation of the mortgaged property;

3. To demand that the mortgagor supply information on the actual conditions of the mortgaged property;

4. To demand that the mortgagor apply necessary measures to preserve the property, the property value in cases where exists the danger of causing the loss or decrease of value of the property due to the exploitation and use thereof;

5. To demand that the mortgagor or a third party that keeps the mortgaged property return such property for disposal in cases where the time for fulfillment of the obligation becomes due while the obligator fails to perform or improperly performs the obligation;

6. To supervise and inspect the process of property formation in case of mortgaging the property to be formed in the future;

7. To request the disposal of the mortgaged property in accordance with the provisions of law.

Rights and obligations of third parties holding mortgaged property

1. A third person holding mortgaged property has the following rights:

a) Exploit the property if so agreed;

b) Receive remuneration and be reimbursed for expenses incurred in taking care of and preserving the mortgaged property, unless otherwise agreed.

2. A third person holding mortgaged property has the following obligations:

a) Take care of and preserve the mortgaged property, and to compensate for any damage if the third person loses the mortgaged property or causes the mortgaged property to lose its value or depreciate in value;

b) Cease the exploitation of the property if it is in danger of losing its value or depreciating in value;

c) Return the mortgaged property to the mortgagee or mortgagor as agreed.

Termination of property mortgage

A property mortgage shall terminate in the following cases:

1. The obligation secured by the mortgage has been terminated;

2. The property mortgage is cancelled or replaced with another security measure;

3. The mortgaged property has been disposed of;

DEPOSIT, SECURITY COLLATERAL, ESCROW ACCOUNT

Deposit

Deposit is an act whereby one party (hereinafter referred to as the depositor) transfers to another party (hereinafter referred to as the depositary) a sum of money or precious metals, gemstones or other valuable things (hereinafter referred to as the deposited property) for a period of time as security for the entering into or performance of a contract.

2. Upon a contract being entered into or performed, any deposited property shall be returned to the depositor, or deducted from the amount of an obligation to pay money. If the depositor refuses to enter into or perform the contract, the deposited property shall belong to the depositary. If the depositary refuses to enter into or perform the contract, it must return the deposited property and pay an amount equivalent to the value of the deposited property to the depositor, unless otherwise agreed.

Security collateral

1. Security collateral is an act whereby a lessee of a movable property transfers a sum of money or precious metals, gems or other valuable things (hereinafter referred to as security collateral property) to the lessor for a specified time limit to secure the return of the leased property.

2. In cases where the leased property is returned, the lessee shall be entitled to reclaim the security collateral property after pay the rental; if the lessee does not return the leased property, the lessor shall be entitled to reclaim the leased property; if the leased property is no longer available for the return, the security collateral property shall belong to the lessor.

Escrow account

1. Escrow account is an act whereby an obligor deposits a sum of money, precious metals, gems or valuable papers into a blocked bank account to secure the performance of a civil obligation.

2. In cases where the obligor has failed to perform or has improperly performed an obligation, the obligee shall be entitled to receive payment and compensation for damage caused by the obligor from the bank where the escrow account is affected, after deducting the bank service charges.

GUARANTEES

Guarantees

1. Guarantee means an undertaking made by a third person (hereinafter referred to as the guarantor) to an obligee (hereinafter referred to as the creditor) to perform an obligation on behalf of an obligor (hereinafter referred to as the principal debtor) if the obligation falls due and the principal fails to perform or performs incorrectly the obligation.

2. The parties may agree that the guarantor shall only be obliged to perform the obligation if the principal debtor is incapable of performing it.

Forms of guarantee

The guarantee must be made in writing, either in a separate document or incorporated in the principal contract.

Scope of guarantees

1. A guarantor may guarantee an obligation in whole or in part on behalf of a principal debtor.

2. A guaranteed obligation includes interest on the principal, penalties and compensation for any damage and interest on late payment, unless otherwise agreed.

3. The parties may agree on using security as property to secure the performance of guaranteed obligation.

4. If the obligation to guarantee is an obligation arising in the future, the scope of guarantee is exclusive of any obligations arising after the guarantor being natural person dies or the guarantor being legal person ceases to exist.

Remuneration

The guarantor shall be entitled to remuneration if so agreed upon between the guarantor and the guaranteed.

Joint guarantors

When more than one person guarantees an obligation, those persons must perform jointly the guarantee, except where it is agreed or provided by law that the guarantee comprises separate portions. The obligee may require any of the joint guarantors to perform the obligation in its entirety.

Where one of the joint guarantors has performed the entire obligation on behalf of the principal debtor, the guarantor may require the other guarantors to perform their respective portions of the obligation with respect to that guarantor.

Relationship between guarantors and creditors

1. If the principal fails to perform or performs incorrectly the obligation, the creditor is entitled to request the guarantor to fulfill the guaranteed obligation, unless contracting parties has agreed that the guarantor only be required to perform the obligation on behalf of the principal debtor in case of the failure to perform obligation by the principal debtor.

2. A creditor may not require a guarantor to perform an obligation on behalf of the principal debtor until the obligation falls due.

3. Where a guarantor is able to offset an obligation with a principal debtor, a guarantor does not have to perform the guaranteed obligation.

Rights to require of guarantors

Each guarantor may require the principal debtor to indemnify the guarantor to the extent of the guarantee, unless otherwise agreed.

Discharge from guaranteed obligations

1. Where the guarantor must perform the guaranteed obligation but the creditor discharges the guarantor from an obligation, the principal debtor is discharged from performance of the obligation with respect to the creditor, except where it is agreed or provided by law.

2. Where one person from amongst the joint guarantors is discharged from the performance of its portion of the guaranteed obligation, the other joint guarantors must, nevertheless, perform their portion of the guaranteed obligation.

3. Where one person from amongst the joint creditors discharge the guarantor from the performance of its portion of the guaranteed obligation, the guarantor must, nevertheless, perform their portion of the guaranteed obligation with respect to remaining joint creditors.

Civil liability of guarantor

1. If the principal debtor fails to perform or perform incorrectly the obligation, the guarantor is obligated to perform such obligation.

2. If the guarantor performs incorrectly the guaranteed obligation, the creditor is entitled to request the guarantor to pay the value of the breached obligation and compensate for any damage.

Termination of guarantees

A guarantee shall terminate in any of the following cases:

1. The obligation secured by the guarantee terminates;

2. The guarantee is cancelled or is substituted by another security;

3. The guarantor has satisfied the guaranteed obligation;

4. As agreed by the parties.

TERMINATION OF CIVIL OBLIGATIONS

Civil liability of guarantor

1. If the principal debtor fails to perform or perform incorrectly the obligation, the guarantor is obligated to perform such obligation.

2. If the guarantor performs incorrectly the guaranteed obligation, the creditor is entitled to request the guarantor to pay the value of the breached obligation and compensate for any damage.

Termination of guarantees

A guarantee shall terminate in any of the following cases:

1. The obligation secured by the guarantee terminates;

2. The guarantee is cancelled or is substituted by another security;

3. The guarantor has satisfied the guaranteed obligation;

4. As agreed by the parties.

Fulfillment of civil obligations

A civil obligation shall be deemed completed when the obligor has performed the entire obligation or part of the obligation but the remaining parts are exempted by the obligee from the performance.

Termination of civil obligations by agreement

Parties may agree to terminate a civil obligation at any time but must not cause damage to the interests of the State or the public or the legal rights or interests of other persons.

Termination of civil obligations due to waiver

1. A civil obligation shall terminate when the obligee waives the obligation of the obligor, unless otherwise provided by law.

2. When a secured civil obligation is waived, the security arrangement shall also terminate.

Termination of a civil obligation by substitution with another civil obligation

1. In cases where the parties agree to substitute the original civil obligation with another civil obligation, the original civil obligation shall terminate.

2. The civil obligation shall also terminate if the obligee has accepted another property or another task as a substitute for the property or the task previously agreed upon.

3. In cases where the civil obligation is an obligation to provide support payment, to pay compensation for damage due to infringement on the life, health, honor, dignity and reputation, or other personal obligation which cannot be transferred to other person, then it shall not be substituted with another obligation.

Termination of civil obligations by offsetting obligations

1. In cases where two parties have reciprocal obligations with respect to properties of the same type and both of which are due, they shall not have to perform obligations to each other and the obligations shall be deemed terminated, except otherwise provided for by law.

2. In cases where the values of the properties or the tasks are different, the parties shall pay the difference in value to each other.

3. Objects which can be valued in money may be used to offset the payment obligation.

Termination of civil obligations when the obligor being an individual dies or being a legal person, or another subject ceases to exist

When it is agreed upon by the parties or provided for by law that the obligation must be performed by the obligor him/her/itself, but such individual has died or the legal person or other subject has ceased to exist, then that obligation shall terminate.

CIVIL CONTRACTS

Definition of civil contract

Civil contract means an agreement between parties in relation to the establishment, modification or termination of civil rights and obligations.

Time when an offer to enter into a civil contract takes effect

1. The time when an offer to enter into a civil contract takes effect shall be determined as follows:

a/ It is fixed by the offeror;

b/ If the offeror does not fix such time, the offer to enter into a civil contract shall take effect from the time the offeree receives such offer.

2. An offer to enter into a contract shall be considered having already been received in the following cases:

a/ The offer is transferred to the place of residence, if the offeree is an individual; to the headquarters, if the offeree is a legal person;

b/ The offer is introduced into the official information system of the offeree;

c/ When the offeree knew the offer to enter into the contract by another mode.

Cancellation of offers to enter into contracts

Where the offeror exercises the right to cancel the offer as such right has been clearly stated in the offer, he/she/it must notify the offeree thereof and such notification shall take effect only when it is received by the offeree before the offeree replies to accept the offer to enter into the contract.

Termination of offers to enter into contracts

An offer to enter into a contract shall terminate in the following cases:

1. The offeree replies not to accept the offer;

2. The time limit for reply of acceptance has expired.

3. When the notice on modication or revocation of the offer takes effect;

4. When the notice on cancellation of the offer takes effect;

5. It is so agreed upon by the offeror and the offeree within the time limit for reply by the offeree

Acceptance of offers to enter into contracts

The acceptance of an offer to enter into a contract is the offeree's reply to the offeror on the acceptance of the whole contents of the offer.

Cases where offerors die or lose their civil act capacity

In cases where the offeror dies or loses his/her civil act capacity after the offeree accepts to enter into the contract, the offer to enter into the contract remains valid.

Cases where offerees die or lose their civil act capacity

In cases where the offeree dies or loses his/her civil act capacity after making his/her reply to accept the offer to enter into the contract, the reply of acceptance to enter into the contract remains valid.

Forms of civil contract

A civil contract can be made orally, in writing or by specific acts.

Contents of civil contracts

Depending on each type of contract, the parties may agree on the following contents:

1. Object of the contract, which is a property to be handed over, or a task to be performed or not to be performed;

2. Quantity and quality;

3. Price and mode of payment;

4. Time limit, place and mode of performing the contract;

5. Rights and obligations of the parties;

6. Liability for breach of contract;

7. Sanction against breach of contract;

Time of entry into civil contracts

1. A civil contract shall be entered into at the time when the offeror receives the reply of acceptance to enter into the contract.

2. A civil contract shall also be considered having been entered into when the time limit for reply has expired and the offeree remains silent, if it is agreed upon by the parties that silence means the reply of acceptance.

3. The time of entry into an oral contract shall be the time at which the parties have agreed on the contents of the contract.

4. The time of entry into a written contract shall be the time at which the last party signs the contract.

Principal types of contracts

Contracts shall have the following main types:

1. Bilateral contract, which is a contract under which a party has the obligation to the other;

2. Unilateral contract, which is a contract under which only one party has the obligation;

3. Principal contract, which is a contract the effect of which does not depend on the auxiliary contract;

4. Auxiliary contract, which is a contract the effect of which depends on the principal contract;

5. Contract for the benefit of a third party, which is a contract under which the contracting parties must perform their obligations and the third party shall enjoy benefits from the performance of such obligations;

6. Conditional contract, which is a contract the performance of which depends on the occurrence, change or termination of a certain event.

Standardized contracts

A standardized contract is a contract which contains provisions prepared by one party according to a standard contract and given to the other party for reply within a reasonable period of time; if the offeree gives its reply of acceptance, he/she/it shall be considered having accepted the entire content of the standardized contract offered by the offeror.

Appendices to contracts

1. Appendices may be attached to a contract to detail some provisions of the contract. Appendices shall be as effective as the contract. The contents of appendices shall not be contrary to the contents of the contract.

2. In cases where appendices contain provisions contrary to the contractual provisions, such provisions shall not be valid, unless otherwise agreed upon. In cases where the parties accept appendices with provisions contrary to contractual provisions, such contractual provisions shall be considered having been amended.

Interpretation of civil contracts

1. When a contract contains ambiguous provisions, the interpretation of such provisions shall be based not only on the wording of the contract but also on the mutual intentions of the parties.

2. When a contractual provision may be construed in several meanings, the meaning which makes the implementation of such provision most beneficial to the parties shall be selected.

3. When a contract contains wordings that may be construed in different meanings, such wordings must be interpreted according to the meaning which is most appropriate to the nature of the contract.

4. When a contract contains a provision or wording that is difficult to understand, such provision or wording must be interpreted according to practices at the place where the contract is entered into.

5. When a contract lacks some provisions, such provisions may be supplemented according to practices at the place where the contract is entered into.

6. The provisions of a contract must be interpreted in relation to each other, so that the meanings of such provisions conform to the whole contents of the contract.

7. In case of contradiction between the mutual intentions of the parties and the contractual wordings, the mutual intentions of the parties shall be used for interpretation of the contract.

8. In cases where the advantageous party includes in the contract the contents unfavorable for the disadvantageous party, the interpretation of the contract must be made along the direction of benefiting the disadvantageous party.

PERFORMANCE OF CONTRACTS

Principles for the performance of civil contracts

The performance of a civil contract must conform to the following principles:

1. It must be performed in accordance with the agreement on the object, quality, quantity, category, time limit, methods and other agreements;

2. It must be performed honestly and in the spirit of cooperation and in a manner that best benefits the parties and ensures mutual trust;

3. It must not infringe upon State interests or legitimate rights and interests of other persons.

Performance of unilateral contracts

With respect to a unilateral contract, the obligor must perform the obligation strictly as agreed. The obligor may only perform the obligation prior to or after the time-limit with the consent of the obligee.

Performance of bilateral contracts

With respect to a bilateral contract, where the parties have agreed on a time limit for the performance of an obligation, each party must perform its obligation when the obligation falls due.

Non-performance of obligations due to the obligee's fault

When a party to a bilateral contract is unable to perform its obligations due to the fault of the other party, the former shall have the right to demand that the other party still perform its obligations toward the former or to cancel the contract and demand compensation for damage.

Failure to perform obligations not due to fault of parties

When a party to a bilateral contract is unable to perform its obligations but the parties are not at fault, the non-performer of the obligations shall have no right to demand that the other party perform its obligations toward him/her/it. In cases where a party has performed part of the obligations, it shall have the right to demand the other party perform the corresponding part of the obligations toward it.

Performance of a contract for the benefit of a third party

When a contract is performed for the benefit of a third party, the third party shall have the right to directly request the obligor to perform the obligation toward it; if there appears a dispute between the parties over the performance of the contract, the third party shall not have the right to demand the performance of the obligation until the dispute is settled.

The obligee may also demand that the obligor perform the contract for the benefit of the third party.

Agreements on fines against violations

1. Agreements on fines for violations are reached by the parties to a contract which requires the violating party to pay a fine to the aggrieved party.

2. The fine levels shall be agreed among the parties.

3. The parties may reach an agreement that the violating party has to pay only a fine for violations and is not liable to any compensation for damage, or has to pay both a fine for violations and a compensation for damage.

AMENDMENT AND TERMINATION OF CONTRACTS

Amendment to contracts

1. The parties may agree to amend their contracts and resolve the consequences of such amendment.

2. Each amended contract must also comply which the formalities of the initial contract.

Termination of contracts

A civil contract shall terminate in any of the following cases:

1. The contract has been fulfilled;

2. It is so agreed upon by the parties;

3. Where a contract is only able to be performed by a particular natural person or legal person having entered into the contract, and that particular natural person dies or that legal person ceases to exist.

4. The contract is cancelled or unilaterally terminated;

5. The contract cannot be performed because its object no longer exists, and the parties may agree to substitute such object with another object or compensate for damage;

Cancellation of contracts

1. A party has the right to cancel a contract and shall not be liable to compensate for damage in any of the following cases:

a) A violation of contract by the other party gives rise to cancellation as agreed by the parties;

b) The other party seriously violates the obligations in the contract;

2. Serious violation means the failure to fulfill obligations properly by a party leading the failure to achieve the purposes of entering into contract by the other party.

3. A party cancelling a contract must notify the other party immediately of the cancellation [and] must compensate if the failure to notify causes damage.

Cancellation of the contract due to late performance of obligations

Where the obligor fails to perform the obligations that the obligee requests in a reasonable period of time but the obligor still fails to perform, the obligee may cancel the contract.

Cancellation of the contract due to inability to perform

Where the obligor cannot perform part or all of its obligations to make the purpose of the obligee may not be reached, the obligee party can cancel the contract and claim damages.

Cancellation of the contract in the case of lost or damaged property

Where a party losses or causes damage to property being the subject of a contract that cannot be refunded or compensated by other property or cannot be repaired or replaced with the same type of property, the other party may cancel contract.

Consequences of cancellation of contracts

1. When a contract is canceled, the contract is void from the time of signing; the parties do not have to fulfill the obligations agreed upon, except for agreement on fines against violations, compensation and settlement of disputes.

2. The parties must return to each other what they have received after deducting from the reasonable costs of contract performance and cost of preservation and development of property.

The refund is made in kind. In case it cannot be returned in kind, it is worth the money to repay.

3. The aggrieved party shall be compensated due to breach of obligations of the other party.

Unilateral termination of performance of contracts

1. A party has the right to terminate unilaterally the performance of a contract without any compensation for damage when a party violates its obligations seriously if so agreed by the parties or so provided by law.

2. A party terminating unilaterally the performance of a contract must notify the other party immediately of its termination of the contract and must compensate if the failure to notify causes damage.

3. Where the performance of a contract is terminated unilaterally, it shall terminate from the time when the other party is notified of the termination. In such case, the parties are not required to continue to perform their obligations, except for agreement on fines for violations, compensation for damage and settlement of disputes. A party which has already performed its obligation may demand the other party to make payment for the performed obligation.

4. The aggrieved party shall receive a compensation for damage caused by the improper performance of obligation by the violating party.

COMMON CIVIL CONTRACTS

CONTRACTS FOR PROPERTY SALE AND PURCHASE

Sale contract of property

Sale contract means an agreement between parties whereby a seller is obligated to transfer the ownership rights of property to the purchaser and the purchaser is obligated to make a payment to the seller.

Objects of sale and purchase contracts

1. The object of a sale and purchase contract shall be a property permitted for transaction.

2. In cases where the object of a sale and purchase contract is an object, that object must be clearly defined.

3. In cases where the object of a sale and purchase contract is a property right, there must be documents of title or other evidence proving such right of the seller.

Quality of objects for sale and purchase contracts

The quality of an object for sale and purchase shall be as agreed by the parties.

Quality of objects for sale and purchase

1. The quality of the objects for sale and purchase shall be agreed upon by the parties.

2. In cases where the quality of objects has been announced or provided for by competent state agencies, the quality of the objects shall be determined in accordance with the announced standards or the regulations of the competent state agencies.

Price and mode of payment

1. The price shall be agreed upon by the parties or determined by a third party at the parties' request.

In cases where the parties agree to make payments at market prices, the price shall be determined at the place and time of payment.

With respect to the property in civil transactions, for which the State has set a price frame, the price shall be agreed upon by the parties in accordance with that price frame.

2. The parties may agree to apply inflation coefficients upon the fluctuation of prices.

3. The agreed price may be a specific price level or a method of determining the price. In cases where the agreement on the price level or the price-determining method is not clear, the price of the property shall be determined, based on the market price at the place and time the contract is entered into.

4. The mode of payment shall be agreed upon by the parties.

Warranty obligation

If agreed by parties or provided by law, a seller has the obligation to provide a warranty for the object for sale and purchase for a certain period, hereinafter referred to as the warranty period.

The warranty period shall be calculated from the time when the purchaser has the obligation to accept the object.

The right to demand warranty

Within the warranty time limit, if the purchaser discovers a defect in the purchased object, he/she/it shall be entitled to request the seller to repair it free of charge, reduce its price, exchange the defective object for another one, or return the object and get back the money.

Compensation for damage within the warranty time limit

1. In addition to the demand for the application of warranty measures, the purchaser shall be entitled to request the seller to compensate for damage caused by technical defects of the object within the warranty time limit.

2. The seller shall not have to compensate for damage if he/she/it can prove that the damage was caused due to the purchaser's fault. The seller shall be entitled to a reduction of damages if the purchaser has not applied the necessary measures within his/her/its capacity to prevent or limit the damage.

CONTRACTS FOR PROPERTY EXCHANGE

Contracts for property exchange

1. A contract for property exchange is an agreement between the parties whereby the parties shall transfer their property and ownership rights to such property to each other.

2. A contract for property exchange must be made in writing, notarized or authenticated or registered, if so provided for by law.

3. In cases where one party exchanges with the other party a property not under its ownership rights or without authorization of the owner, the other party shall be entitled to cancel the contract and demand compensation for damage.

4. Each party shall be considered the seller of the property transferred to the other party and the buyer of the property received.

Payment for differences in value

In cases where the exchanged property has differences in value, the parties must pay each other for such differences, unless otherwise agreed upon or provided for by law.

CONTRACTS FOR GIFTS OF PROPERTY

Contracts for gifts of property

Contract for a gift of property means an agreement between parties whereby the giver delivers its property and transfers its ownership rights to the recipient without requiring compensation and the recipient agrees to accept the gift.

Liability in respect of intentional gift of property not under one's ownership

Where a giver intentionally gives property which is not under its ownership and the recipient does not know or is not able to know, such giver must reimburse the recipient for expenses incurred by the recipient in increasing the value of the property at such time as it is reclaimed by the owner.

CONTRACTS FOR LOAN OF PROPERTY

Contracts for loan of property

Contract for the loan of property means an agreement between parties whereby a lender delivers property to a borrower. When the loan falls due, the borrower must repay the lender property of the same type in accordance with the correct quantity and quality, and must pay interest if so agreed.

Ownership rights with respect to property lent

A borrower shall become the owner of borrowed property from the time of delivery of the property.

Obligations of the lender

The lender shall have the following obligations:

1. To hand over to the borrower the property in full, of the right quality and in the right quantity at the time and place agreed upon.

2. To compensate for damage to the borrower if the lender is aware that the property is not of the required quality but fails to notify the borrower thereof, except in cases where the borrower is aware thereof but still receives such property;

3. Not to request the borrower to return the property ahead of time.

Use of borrowed property

Parties may agree that borrowed property may only be used for the agreed purpose of the loan. The lender may check the use of the property and may demand its early return if, despite warning, the borrower continues to use the property contrary to the agreed purpose.

Performance of contracts for loans without fixed term

1. With respect to a contract for an interest-free loan without a fixed term, the lender may reclaim the property, and the borrower may repay the debt, at any time provided that each party gives reasonable prior notice to the other party, unless otherwise agreed.

2. With respect to a contract for a loan with interest without a fixed term, the lender may reclaim the property at any time, subject to giving reasonable prior notice to the borrower, and shall be paid interest until the time when the property is returned. The borrower may also return the property at any time, subject to giving reasonable prior notice to the lender, in which case the borrower shall pay interest only up to the date on which repayment is made.

Performance of contracts for fixed term loans

1. With respect to a contract for a fixed term interest-free loan, the borrower may return the property at any time, subject to giving reasonable prior notice to the lender. The lender may reclaim the property prior to the due date, subject to the consent of the borrower.

2. With respect to a contract for a fixed term loan with interest, the borrower may return the property prior to the due date, but must pay interest for the entire term, unless otherwise agreed.

CONTRACTS FOR PROPERTY LEASE

Contracts for property lease

A contract for property lease is an agreement between the parties whereby the lessor shall hand over the property to the lessee for use for a specified period of time, and the lessee must pay a rent.

Sub-leases

A lessee may sub-lease leased property with the consent of the lessor.

Delivery of leased property

1. A lessor must deliver property to the lessee strictly in accordance with the agreed quantity, quality, type and condition and at the agreed place and time, and must provide information necessary for use of the property.

2. Where a lessor is late in delivering property, the lessee may extend the time for the delivery of the property or may cancel the contract and demand compensation for damage. If the leased property is not of the quality agreed, the lessee has the right to require the lessor to repair the property or reduce the rent, or to cancel the contract and demand compensation for damage.

Obligation to assure right of lessees to use property

1. A lessor must assure the right of a lessee to uninterfered use of the property.

2. In the event of a dispute as to the ownership rights with respect to leased property, which interferes with use of that property by the lessee, the lessee has the right to terminate unilaterally the performance of the contract and demand compensation for damage.

Obligation to take care of leased property

1. A lessee shall take care of leased property as if it were its own and shall carry out minor repairs and maintenance. If the lessee causes any loss of or damage to the property, it must compensate the lessor.

The lessee shall not be liable for normal wear and tear due to the use of the leased property.

2. A lessee may, with the consent of the lessor, carry out repairs and improvements to leased property which increase its value and may require reimbursement from the lessor for reasonable costs incurred.

Obligation to use leased property strictly in accordance with utility and purpose

1. A lessee must use leased property strictly in accordance with its utility and the agreed purpose.

2. Where a lessee fails to use leased property strictly in accordance with its utility and purpose, the lessor has the right to terminate unilaterally the performance of the contract and to demand compensation for damage.

Payment of rent

A lessee must pay rent in full and on time as agreed.

Return of leased property

A lessee must return leased property in the same condition in which it was received, normal wear and tear excepted, or in the condition agreed. If the value of the leased property has decreased in comparison with its condition at the time it was received, the lessor has the right to demand compensation for any damage, normal wear and tear excepted.

CONTRACTS FOR PACKAGE LEASES OF PROPERTY

Contracts for package leases of property

A contract for a package lease of property is an agreement between the parties whereby the package lessor hands over the property to the lessee for the exploitation of its utility and the enjoyment of the yields and profits gained from such property and the lessee has the obligation to pay the rent.

Objects of package lease contracts

Objects of a contract for a package lease of property may be land, forest, unexploited water surface, animals, production and/or business establishments, other means of production as well as necessary equipment and facilities for exploiting the utility, enjoying the yields or profits, unless otherwise provided for by law.

Package lease term

The package lease term shall be agreed upon by the parties according to the production and/or business cycle consistent with the characteristics of the object of the package lease.

Package lease price

The package lease price shall be agreed upon by the parties.

Return of package lease property

Upon the termination of a package lease contract, the lessee must return the package lease property in the conditions corresponding to the agreed depreciation level; if the lessee causes loss or reduction of the value of the package lease property, he/she/it must compensate for the damage.

CONTRACTS FOR PROPERTY BORROWING

Contracts for property borrowing

A contract for property borrowing is an agreement between the parties whereby the lender hands over the property to the borrower for use in a specified time limit free of charge, and the borrower must return such property when the borrowing term ends or the borrowing purpose has been achieved.

Objects of property-borrowing contracts

Everything that is non-expendable may be object of a contract for borrowing a property.

Obligations of the property borrower

The property borrower shall have the following obligations:

1. To preserve and maintain the borrowed property as if it were his/her/its own property; not to change the conditions of the borrowed property on his/her/its own will; if the property suffers normal damage, it must be repaired;

2. Not to sub-lend the borrowed property without the lender's consent;

3. To return the borrowed property on time; if there is no agreement on the deadline for the return of the property, the borrower must return it immediately after the borrowing purpose has been achieved;

4. To compensate for damage if he/she/it causes any damage to, or loss of, the borrowed property.

Rights of the property borrower

The property borrower shall have the following rights:

1. To use the borrowed property in accordance with its utility and the agreed purpose;

2. To request the lender to reimburse the reasonable expenses for any repair or for increasing the value of the borrowed property, if so agreed upon.

3. Not to be liable for natural wear of the borrowed property.

Obligations of the property lender

The property lender shall have the following obligations:

1. To provide necessary information on the use of the property and defects of the property, if any;

2. To reimburse to the borrower expenses for repair, expenses for increasing the value of the borrowed property, if so agreed upon;

3. To compensate the borrower for any damage, if the lender knows about the defects of the property but does not inform the borrower thereof, thus causing damage to the borrower, except for the defects which the borrower knew or should have known.

Rights of the property lender

The property lender shall have the following rights:

1. To reclaim the property immediately after the borrower has achieved his/her purpose, if there is no agreement on the borrowing period; if the lender has urgent and unexpected needs to use the lent property, he/she/its shall be entitled to reclaim the property even if the borrower has not yet achieved his/her/its purpose, but must notify the borrower thereof in advance within a reasonable period of time;

2. To reclaim the property when the borrower does not use the property for the right purpose, in accordance with its utility or the agreed method or the borrower sublends the property without the lender's consent;

3. To demand compensation for damage caused to the property by the borrower.

COOPERATION CONTRACT

Cooperation contract

1. A cooperation contract means an agreement between natural and/or legal persons regarding the property contribution, effort to perform certain jobs, the same benefit and mutual responsibility.

2. Each cooperation contract must be made in writing.

Contents of cooperation contract

Each cooperation contract shall contain the major contents below:

1. Purpose and duration of cooperation;

2. Full name and place of residence of natural person; name and headquarters of legal person;

3. Contributed property (if any);

4. Contributed labor (if any);

5. Method of distributing the yield and/or income;

6. Rights and obligations of cooperative members;

7. Rights and obligations of representatives (if any);

8. Conditions for participation and withdrawal from the cooperation contract (if any);

9. Conditions for termination of cooperation.

Termination of cooperation contract

1. A cooperation contract shall terminate in any of the following cases:

a) As agreed by cooperative members;

b) The time limit mentioned in the cooperation contract has expired;

c) The purpose of cooperation has been achieved;

2. Upon the termination of the cooperation contract, the debts arising from the contract must be paid;

Where the debt was repaid and the common property still exists, it shall be divided by the cooperative members in proportion to the contribution of each person, unless otherwise agreed.

SERVICE CONTRACTS

Service contracts

A service contract means an agreement between parties whereby a service provider performs an act for a client which pays a fee for that act.

Objects of service contracts

The object of a contract for services must be an act which is capable of being performed, which is not prohibited by law.

Obligations of the service hirer (client)

The service hirer (client) shall have the following obligations:

1. To supply the service provider with necessary information, documents and means for the performance of the task, if so agreed upon or so required by the performance of the task;

2. To pay service charges to the service provider as agreed upon.

Rights of the service hirer (client)

The service hirer (client) shall have the following rights:

1. To request the service provider to perform the task in accordance with the agreed quality, quantity, time limit, location and other agreements;

2. In cases where the service provider violates its obligations, the service hirer (client) shall have the right to unilaterally terminate the performance of the contract and demand compensation for damage.

Obligations of the service provider

The service provider shall have the following obligations:

1. To perform the task in accordance with the agreed quality, quantity, time limit, location and other agreements;

2. Not to assign other persons to perform the task without the service hirer (client)'s consent;

3. To preserve and return to the service hirer (client) the supplied documents and means after fulfillment of the task;

4. To immediately notify the service hirer (client) of any inadequacy of information and documents and poor quality of the means for fulfilling the task;

5. To keep secret the information which he/she/it has come to know during the time of providing the service, if so agreed upon or provided for by law;

6. To compensate the service hirer (client) for damage, if he/she/it causes the loss of, or damage to, the supplied documents and/or means or discloses secret information.

Rights of the service provider

The service provider shall have the following rights:

1. To request the service hirer (client) to supply necessary information, documents and means;

2. To change the service conditions in the interests of the service hirer (client) without necessarily having to wait for the opinion of the service hirer (client), if such wait may cause damage to the service hirer (client), but the service provider must immediately notify the service hirer (client) thereof;

3. To request the service hirer (client) to pay the service charges.

TRANSPORT CONTRACTS

Contracts for transport of passengers

A contract for transportation of passengers is an agreement between the parties whereby the carrier shall transport the passenger and his/her luggage to the specified destination as agreed upon, and the passenger shall have to pay the transportation fare.

Forms of contract for transportation of passengers

1. A contract for transportation of passengers may be made in writing or orally.

2. Tickets shall be the evidence of the entry into a contract for transportation of passengers between the parties.

Obligations of the carrier

The carrier shall have the following obligations:

1. To transport the passengers from the place of departure to the place of destination on time, in a civilized and courteous manner and safely by the agreed means and prescribed route; provide sufficient seats for passengers and not transport in excess of the prescribed load;

2. To buy civil liability insurance for passengers as provided for by law;

3. To ensure the departure time as notified or agreed upon;

4. To transport luggage and return them to the passengers or to the persons entitled to receive such luggage at the agreed place and time along the route as agreed upon;

5. To reimburse the transportation fare to the passengers as agreed upon or provided for by law.

Rights of the carrier

The carrier shall have the following rights:

1. To request passengers to pay in full the transportation fares and charges for the transport of accompanied luggage in excess of the prescribed limit.

2. To refuse to transport a passenger in the following cases:

a/ Where the passenger fails to comply with the regulations of the carrier or commits acts of causing public disorder, hindering the work of the carrier, threatening the life, health or property of other persons or commits other acts threatening the safety of the journey; in this case. the passenger shall not be refunded the transportation fare and must be fined for violation, if so provided for by the transport regulations;

b/ Where the carrier clearly sees that due to the health condition of the passenger, the transportation may cause danger to the passenger him/herself or others during the journey;

c/ To prevent the spread of epidemics.

Obligations of the passenger

The passenger shall have the following obligations:

1. To pay fully the passenger transportation fare and the charge for the transport of luggage in excess of the prescribed limit, and take care of his/her luggage by him/herself;

2. To be present at the place of departure on the agreed time;

3. To respect and strictly observe the regulations of the carrier and other regulations on traffic safety.

Rights of the passenger

The passenger shall have the following rights:

1. Request to be transported by the agreed means of transport, in the class commensurate with the value of the ticket and in accordance with the agreed route.

2. Be exempt from transport fares for check-in luggage and hand-luggage within the limits as agreed or as provided by law.

3. Demand reimbursement of expenses incurred or compensation for any damage if the carrier is at fault in failing to transport according to the agreed time schedule and destination.

4. Receive the luggage at the agreed destination in accordance with the agreed time and route.

CONTRACTS FOR TRANSPORTATION OF PROPERTY

Contracts for transportation of property

A contract for transportation of property is an agreement between the parties whereby the carrier shall have the obligation to carry the property to the specified place as agreed upon and hand over such property to the person entitled to receive it and the transport hirer shall have the obligation to pay the freight.

Forms of contract for transportation of property

1. A contract for transportation of property shall be made orally or in writing.

2. The bill of lading or other equivalent transportation documents shall be the evidence of the entry into contracts between the parties.

Obligations of the carrier

The carrier shall have the following obligations:

1. To ensure that the property is transported in full and safely to the designated place and on time;

2. To hand over the property to the person entitled to receive it;

3. To bear the costs related to the transportation of the property, unless otherwise agreed upon;

4. To buy civil liability insurance as provided for by law;

5. To compensate the transport hirer in cases where the carrier causes the loss of, or damage to, the property due to the carrier's fault, unless otherwise agreed upon or provided for by law.

Rights of the carrier

The carrier shall have the following rights:

1. To check the authenticity of the property and the bill of lading or other equivalent transport documents;

2. To refuse to carry any property of types other than those agreed upon in the contracts;

3. To request the transport hirer to pay freight in full and on schedule;

4. To refuse to carry the property banned from transaction, dangerous and/or noxious property, if the carrier knows or should have known such;

5. To demand compensation for damage from the transport hirer.

Obligations of the transport hirer

The transport hirer shall have the following obligations:

1. To pay in full the freight charges to the carrier, at the time and by the method of payment as agreed.

2. To provide necessary information about the transported property to ensure its safety.

3. To take care of the property during transport if so agreed. Where the customer takes care of the property and it is lost or damaged, the customer shall not be entitled to compensation.

Rights of the transport hirer

The transport hirer shall have the following rights:

1. To request the carrier to transport the property to the agreed place and at the agreed time;

2. To personally receive back or appoint a third party to receive back the property the transport of which is hired;

3. To demand compensation for damage from the carrier.

PROCESSING CONTRACTS

Processing contracts

Processing contract means an agreement between parties whereby a processor carries out work to create products at the request of a supplier, and the supplier receives the products and pays fees.

Subject matter of processing contracts

The subject matter of a processing contract shall be items which are specified by samples, the standard of which is agreed by the parties.

Obligation of suppliers

1. Supply raw materials to the processor strictly in accordance with the agreed quantity, quality, time and place, unless otherwise agreed by the parties; and to provide necessary documents relating to the processing.

2. Provide the processor with instructions as to how to perform the contract.

3. Pay agreed fees.

Rights of suppliers

1. Accept the processed products in accordance with the agreed quantity, quality, manner, time and place.

2. Terminate unilaterally performance of the contract and demand compensation for damage if the processor commits a serious breach of the contract.

3. Where the products are not of the agreed quality and the supplier accepts the products but requests repairs, but the processor is not able to perform the repairs within the agreed time, the supplier has the right to cancel the contract and demand compensation for damage.

Obligations of processors

1. Take care of the raw materials supplied by the supplier.

2. Notify the supplier to replace any raw materials supplied which are not of the agreed quality; to refuse to perform the processing if the use of the raw materials may create products which pose a danger to society.

3. Deliver the products to the supplier strictly in accordance with the agreed quantity, quality, method, time and place.

4. Keep confidential all information relating to the processing and the products.

5. Bear liability for the quality of the products, unless the lack of quality is due to the raw materials supplied by the supplier or due to the unreasonable instructions of the supplier.

6. Return any leftover raw materials to the supplier after completing performance of the contract.

Rights of processors

1. Require the supplier to deliver the raw materials strictly in accordance with the agreed quality, quantity, time and place.

2. Refuse to comply with unreasonable instructions of the supplier where the processor is of the view that [compliance with] such instructions could decrease the quality of the products provided that the processor immediately informs the supplier.

3. Require the supplier to make payment of the fees in full, at the time and by the method as agreed.

CONTRACTS FOR BAILMENT OF PROPERTY

Contracts for bailment of property

Contract for bailment of property means an agreement between parties whereby a bailee accepts the property of a bailor for safekeeping, for return to the bailor upon expiry of the duration of the contract, and the bailor must pay a fee to the bailee, except where the bailment is free of charge.

Obligation of bailors of property

1. Inform the bailee of the condition of the property and the appropriate safekeeping measures upon delivery of the property; if the bailor fails to inform the bailee, and the property is destroyed or damaged as a result of inappropriate safekeeping, the bailor must be liable itself for such destruction of or damage to the bailed property and must compensate for other damage caused.

2. Pay the bailment fees in full, at the time and by the method as agreed.

Rights of bailors of property

1. Reclaim the property at any time subject to giving reasonable prior notice to the bailee if the bailment contract does not specify a period of time.

2. Demand compensation for loss of or damage to the bailed property caused by the bailee, except in the case of an event of force majeure.

Obligation of bailees of property

1. Take care of the property as agreed and return it to the bailor in the same condition in which the bailee received it.

2. Change the method for safekeeping of the property only where such change is necessary for better safekeeping of such property and provided that the bailor is notified immediately of the change.

3. Notify promptly the bailor in writing and request the bailor to advise, within a certain period of time, a solution where, due to its nature, the bailed property is in danger of being damaged or destroyed. If the bailor fails to reply within such period of time, the bailee has the right to take all necessary measures to take care of the property and to require the bailee to reimburse the costs incurred.

4. Compensate for damage where the bailee causes any loss of or damage to the bailed property, except in the case of an event of force majeure.

Rights of bailees of property

1. Require the bailor to pay the agreed bailment fees.

2. Require the bailor to pay the reasonable costs of taking care of the property where the bailment is free of charge.

3. Request, at any time, the bailor to take back the property subject to giving reasonable prior notice to the bailor where the bailment is for an indefinite period of time.

4. Sell the property in the interests of the bailor where the bailed property is in danger of being damaged or destroyed, inform the bailor thereof and pay the proceeds of the sale to the bailor after deduction of reasonable expenses incurred for the sale of the property.

AUTHORIZATION CONTRACTS

Authorization contracts

Authorization contract means an agreement between parties whereby an attorney has the obligation to perform an act in the name of a principal. The principal shall only be required to pay remuneration if so agreed or so provided by law.

Obligation of attorneys

1. Perform the act in accordance with the authorization and inform the principal of such performance.

2. Notify any third parties involved in the performance of the authorized act of the duration and scope of the authorization and of any amendments of or additions to such scope.

3. Take care of and preserve documents and facilities provided for the performance of the authorized act.

4. Keep all information confidential which the attorney comes to know during the performance of the authorized act.

5. Return to the principal any property received and benefits derived during the performance of the authorized act as agreed or as provided by law.

6. Compensate for damage caused by a breach of any of the obligations.

Rights of attorneys

1. Require the principal to provide the information, documentation and facilities necessary for performance of the authorized act.

2. Receive remuneration and be reimbursed for reasonable expenses incurred in the performance of the authorized act.

Obligation of principals

1. Provide the information, documentation and facilities necessary for the attorney to perform the authorized act.

2. Be liable for undertakings given by the attorney within the scope of the authorization.

3. Reimburse the attorney for reasonable expenses incurred by the attorney in the performance of the authorized act and pay any agreed remuneration to the attorney.

Rights of principals

1. Require the attorney to report fully on the performance of the authorized act.

2. Require the attorney to return any property and benefits derived from the performance of the authorized act, unless otherwise agreed.

3. Compensate for damage caused by a breach of any of the obligations.

INHERITANCE

Inheritance right of individuals

Every individual shall have the right to make a testament to dispose of his/her property; to bequeath his/her property to his/her heir(s) at law; and to inherit property under a testament or according to law.

Individuals' right of equality in inheritance

Every individual shall be equal in the right to bequeath his/her property to another person and the right to inherit property under a testament or according to law.

Time and place of commencing inheritance

The time of commencement of an inheritance shall be the time when the deceased dies.

Estates

An estate comprises property which the deceased owned and property which the deceased jointly owned with other persons.

Heirs

If an heir is an individual, he/she must be alive at the time of opening the inheritance, or must be born and still alive after the time of opening the inheritance, but must be conceived before the death of the estate leaver.

Testaments/ Wills

A testament is the expression of an individual's will to transfer his/her own property to other person(s) after his/her death.

Testators

A person who has attained adulthood is entitled to make a testament, except in cases where such person is affected by a mental disease or other ailment, which prevents him/her from being aware of, or controlling his/her acts.

Rights of the testator

The testator shall have the following rights:

1. To designate his/her heirs(s); to disinherit an heir;

2. To divide his/her estate for each of his/her heirs;

3. To set aside part of his/her estate for donation and/or worship;

4. To assign obligations to his/her heir(s);

5. To designate a person to keep the testament, the administrator of his/her estate and the distributor of the estate.

Forms of testament

A testament must be made in writing; if the testament cannot be made in writing, it can be made orally.

Written testaments

A written testament may be:

1. A written testament made without witnesses;

2. A written testament made in the presence of witnesses;

3. A notarized written testament;

4. An authenticated written testament.

Oral testaments

In cases where a human life is threatened by a disease or other causes, which prevent him/her from making a written testament, he/she may make an oral testament.

Lawful testaments

A testament shall be considered lawful when it meets all the following conditions:

a/ The testator is clear-minded while making the testament; he/she is not deceived, threatened or forced;

b/ The content of the testament is not contrary to law; the form of testament is not contrary to the provisions of law.

Contents of written testaments

A testament must contain:

a/ Day, month, year, on which the testament is made;

b/ Full name and place of residence of the testator;

c/ Full names of the person(s), agency(ies) or organization(s) entitled to the estate or the clear definition of conditions for individuals, agencies or organizations to enjoy the estate;

d/ The inheritance estate bequeathed and the location of such estate;

e/ The person(s) appointed to perform the obligations and the contents of such obligations.

Amendment of, addition to, replacement or revocation of wills

1. A testator may amend, add to, replace or revoke his or her will at any time.

2. Where a testator replaces a will with a new will, the previous will shall be deemed to have been revoked.

CIVIL PROCEDURE

Task of the Civil Procedure Law

The Civil Procedure Code provides for the basic principles in civil proceedings; the order and procedures for initiating lawsuits at courts to settle cases of civil, marriage and family, business, trade and labor disputes; the order and procedures for settlement of civil cases and matters at courts; the civil judgment enforcement; the tasks, powers and responsibilities of the procedure-conducting agencies, the procedure-conducting persons;

BASIC PRINCIPLES

Compliance with laws in civil procedures

All civil procedural activities of procedure-conducting persons, civil procedure-participants, of relevant individuals, agencies and organizations must comply with the provisions of law.

Right to request Courts to protect legitimate rights and interests

Individuals, agencies and organizations shall have the right to institute civil lawsuits, request the resolution of civil matters at competent Courts in order to protect the justice, human's rights, civil rights, benefits of the State, legitimate rights and interests of their own or of others.

Supply of evidences and proof in civil procedures

The involved parties shall have the right and obligation to initiatively collect and supply evidence to Courts and prove that their petitions are well grounded and lawful.

Agencies, organizations and individuals initiating lawsuits or file their petitions to protect legitimate rights and interests of their own or of other persons shall have the right and obligation to collect and supply evidence and to prove the ground and the lawfulness like the involved parties.

Responsibility of competent individuals, agencies and organizations to supply materials and evidences

Agencies, organizations and individuals shall, within the scope of their tasks and powers, provide the involved parties, the Courts with materials and evidences currently being under their possession or management sufficiently and timely at the petition of the involved parties, the Courts.

Equality in rights and obligations in civil procedures

All citizens are equal before law and courts regardless of their social status, beliefs, nationalities, sexes, religions, occupations and educational levels.

Ensuring the involved parties' right to protect legitimate rights and interests

The involved parties have the right to defend themselves or to ask lawyers to protect their legitimate rights and interests.

Mediation in civil procedures

The Courts have the responsibility to conduct mediation and create favorable conditions for the involved parties to reach agreement with one another.

PARTICIPANTS IN CIVIL PROCEDURES

Involved parties in civil cases

1. The involved parties in civil lawsuits are agencies, organizations and individuals, including the plaintiffs, the defendants and the persons with related interests and obligations.

2. The litigator in a civil lawsuit is the person that initiates lawsuit or the person for whom the other agencies, organizations and individuals initiates the lawsuit to request the Court to resolve the civil lawsuit when he/she holds that the legitimate rights and interests of that person have been infringed upon.

3. The defendant in a civil lawsuit is the person against whom the plaintiff initiates a lawsuit or the other agencies, organizations and individuals prescribed by this Code initiates a lawsuit to request the Court to resolve the civil lawsuit when they hold that the legitimate rights and interests of the plaintiff have been infringed upon by such person.

Rights and obligations of the involved parties

The involved parties shall have equal rights and obligations when participating in civil procedures. When participating in civil procedures, the involved parties shall have the following rights and obligations:

1. To respect courts, and strictly observe the court's rules;

2. To advance Court fees and charges and pay Court fees and charges and other expenses as prescribed by law;

3. To provide sufficiently and accurately address of their residence/work place;

4. To maintain, modify, supplement or withdraw their petitions;

5. To supply materials and evidences; to prove to protect their legitimate rights and interests;

6. To petition agencies, organizations and individuals that are keeping or managing materials and evidences to supply such materials and evidences to them;

7. To petition the Court to verify and collect materials and evidences of the cases which they cannot perform themselves; petition the Court to request other involved parties to present materials and evidences they are keeping; petition the Court to issue the decision to request the agencies, organizations and individuals that are keeping and managing the materials/evidences to supply such materials and evidences; request the Court to summon witnesses, to ask for expertise, evaluation or price appraisal;

8. To read and take notes, make photocopies of materials and evidences produced by other involved parties or collected by courts.

9. To reach agreement with one another on the resolution of cases: to participate in mediation conducted by courts;

10. To receive regular notices for the exercise of their rights and obligations;

11. To protect by themselves or ask other persons to protect their legitimate rights and interests;

12. To petition the replacement of civil proceeding officers or participants in civil procedures in accordance with this Code;

13. To argue in Court sessions, to present argument about assessment of the evidence and the applied law provisions;

14. To be provided with extracts of Court judgments, judgments or decisions;

Defense counsels of involved parties' legitimate rights and interests

The defense counsels of involved parties' legitimate rights and interests are persons who participate in the procedures to protect the involved parties' legitimate rights and interests

Rights and obligations of defense counsels of the involved parties' legitimate rights and interests

1. To participate in the procedures right at the time of lawsuit initiation or at any stage in the civil procedures.

2. To collect and supply materials and evidences to courts; to study case files and to take notes, to copy necessary materials in the case files in order to defend the legitimate rights and interests of the involved parties.

3. To participate in mediation, Court sessions or make their written defense of the legitimate rights and interests of the involved parties to Courts for consideration.

4. To provide involved parties with legal aid related to the defense of their legitimate rights and interests.

Witnesses

Persons who know details related to the contents of cases may be summoned by Courts at the request of the involved parties to participate in the procedures in the capacity as witnesses. Persons who lose their civil act capacity cannot act as witnesses.

Rights and obligations of witnesses

1. To supply all information, documents and/or objects they have obtained, which are related to the resolution of cases.

2. To honestly declare details they know, which are related to the resolution of cases.

3. To be paid related expenses according to law provisions.

4. To petition the Courts which have summoned them and competent agencies to protect their lives, health, honor, dignity, properties and other legitimate rights and interests when participating in the procedures;

5. To compensate and take legal responsibility for damage caused to the involved parties or other persons by their untruthful testimonies.

PROOFS AND EVIDENCES

Evidences

Evidences in civil cases are factual things which are handed to Courts by involved parties, agencies, organizations or individuals.

Sources of evidence

Evidences are gathered from the following sources:

1. Readable, audible or visible materials, electronic data;

2. Exhibits;

3. Involved parties' testimonies;

4. Witnesses' testimonies;

5. Expertising conclusions;

6. On-site appraisal minutes;

7. Property evaluation and price appraisal results;

8. Written records of legal facts or acts that are formulated by functional persons;

9. Notarized/authenticated documents;

INSTITUTION AND ACCEPTANCE OF CASES

Right to institute cases

Agencies, organizations and individuals are entitled to institute cases by themselves or through their lawful representatives (hereinafter referred to as the litigators) at competent.

Accepting cases

After receiving lawsuit petitions and accompanied materials and/or evidences, if deeming that the cases fall within the courts' jurisdiction, the Judges shall immediately notify the litigators thereof so that they may come to Courts for carrying out procedures to advance the Court fees in cases where they are liable thereto.

Suspension of the resolution of civil lawsuits

The Court shall issue a decision to suspend the resolution of a civil lawsuit in one of the following cases:

a) The involved parties being individuals have died;

b) One involved party being an individual has lost his/her civil act capacity or being a minor while his/her representative at law has not been determined yet;

c) The lawful representative of an involved party terminates without a replacement;

Termination of the resolution of civil lawsuits

After accepting cases which fall within their respective jurisdiction, the Courts shall issue decisions to terminate the resolution of the civil lawsuits in the following circumstances:

a) The plaintiffs or defendants being individuals have died while their rights and obligations are not inherited;

b) Agencies or organizations have been dissolved or are bankrupt without any agencies, organizations or individuals inheriting their procedural rights and obligations;

c) The litigators withdraw all petitions for initiation of lawsuits;

Procedures for rendering Court judgments or decisions in Court sessions

1. Judgments must be discussed and adopted by the Trial Panels in the deliberation rooms.

2. Decisions to replace the procedure presiding officers, expert-witnesses, interpreters, to transfer the cases, to suspend or terminate the resolution of cases, or to postpone Court sessions, or decisions to recognize the agreement between involved parties or to suspend the Court session, must be discussed and adopted by the trial panel at the deliberation rooms and made in writing.

Recognizing the agreements of involved parties

The presiding Judge of the Court shall ask if the involved parties can reach an agreement about the case resolution. If the involved parties can voluntarily reach an agreement on the case resolution that is not contrary the law or social ethics, the trial panel shall issue decisions on recognition of the agreement between involved parties on the case resolution

Contents and mode of oral argument in Court sessions

1. Oral argument at the Courts include the presentation of evidences, questioning and answering and the expression of opinions and argument about evidences and details of the civil lawsuits or disputes and the applicable law provisions for the resolution of petitions of involved parties in the cases.

2. The oral argument at the Courts shall be conducted according to the direction of the Presiding Judge of the Court session.

3. The Presiding Judge must not limit the duration of the oral argument and must enable persons who participate in the argument to present fully their opinions;

DELIBERATION AND PRONOUNCEMENT OF JUDGMENTS

Deliberation

1. At the end of arguments, the trial panels enter the deliberation rooms to deliberate the cases.

2. During the deliberation, the trial panel members must base themselves on materials and evidences examined at the Court sessions, the results of arguments at the Court sessions and law provisions;

Pronouncing judgments

The Trial panels shall pronounce the judgments in the presence of involved parties, representatives of agencies/organizations/individuals initiating lawsuits.

If the involved parties need interpreters, the interpreters shall interpret the parts of judgment that are publicly pronounced.

PROCEDURES FOR RESOLUTION OF CASES AT APPELLATE COURTS

Nature of appellate trial

Appellate trial means the re-trial by the appellate Court of a case with the first-instance court's judgment or decision having not yet taken legal effect and being appealed against.

Persons having the right to appeal

The involved parties or their representatives, agencies, organizations or individuals initiating lawsuits shall have the right to lodge their appeals against judgments or decisions of the first-instance Courts in order to request the appellate Courts to conduct re-trials according to the appellate procedures.

APPELLATE TRIAL PROCEDURES

Scope of appellate trial

The appellate Courts shall only review the parts of the first-instance judgments/decisions, which are appealed against or related to the review of the appealed contents.

Participants in appellate Court sessions

The appellants, the involved parties, agencies/organizations/individuals that are related to the resolution of the appeals and the defense counsels of the involved parties' legitimate rights and interests must be summoned to the appellate Court sessions.

Arguments in appellate Court sessions

In appellate Court sessions, involved parties and defense counsels of legitimate rights and interests of involved parties shall argue only about matters falling within the scope of appellate trials that have been inquired in appellate Court sessions.

CASSATION PROCEDURES

Nature of cassation

Cassation means the review of courts' legally effective judgments or decisions, which are appealed against when there is one of the following grounds:

a) Conclusion in the judgment/decision is incompatible with the objective details of the cases, causing damage to legitimate rights and interests of the involved parties;

b) There are serious violations against procedures that prevent involved parties from executing their procedural rights and obligations, as the result, their legitimate rights and interests are not protected as prescribed in law;

c) There are mistakes in the application of law leading to the issuance of wrong judgments/decisions, causing bad effect to legitimate rights and interests of involved parties, infringing upon public benefits, State benefits, legitimate rights and interests of the third parties.

Jurisdiction of the Cassation Review Panels

The Cassation Review Panels shall have the following powers:

1. To reject the appeals and uphold the court's legally effective judgments/decisions;

2. To repeal the legally effective judgments/decisions of Courts and uphold the lawful judgments/decisions of the subordinate courts, which have been annulled or amended;

3. To repeal parts or the whole of courts' legally effective judgments/decisions to retry according to first-instance procedures or appellate procedures;

4. To repeal legally effective judgments/decisions and terminate the resolution of the cases;

5. To modify parts or the whole of the legally effective judgments/decisions.

REOPENING PROCEDURES

Nature of reopening procedures

Reopening means the review of legally effective judgments/decisions which are appealed against due to the appearance of newly detected details which may substantially change the contents of the judgments/decisions and about which the Courts and involved parties did not know when the Courts rendered such judgments or decisions.

Grounds for appeal according to reopening procedures

Legally effective judgments/decisions shall be appealed against according to reopening procedures when there is one of the following grounds:

1. Important details of the case were newly discovered which the involved parties could not have known in the course of resolving the case;

2. There are grounds to prove that the conclusions of the expert witnesses and translations of interpreters were untruthful or evidences were falsified;

3. The criminal, administrative, civil, marriage and family, business, commercial or labor judgments/decisions of Courts or decisions of State agencies on which the Courts based themselves to resolve the cases had already been annulled.

Conclusion

Thank you again for downloading this book on *"CIVIL LAW: Mastering Essential Legal Terms Explained About Civil Rights, Guardianship, Civil Transactions, Civil Obligations, Civil Liability, Civil Contracts and Civil Procedure!"* and reading all the way to the end. I'm extremely grateful.

If you know of anyone else who may benefit from the informative legal words presented in this book, please help me inform them of this book. I would greatly appreciate it.

Finally, if you enjoyed this book and feel that it has added value to your study or career in any way, please take a couple of minutes to share your thoughts and post a REVIEW on Amazon. Your feedback will help me to continue to write the kind of Kindle books that helps you get results. Furthermore, if you write a simple REVIEW with positive words for this book on Amazon, you can help hundreds or perhaps thousands of other readers who may want to enhance their legal vocabulary have a chance getting what they need. Like you, they worked hard for every penny they spend on books. With the information and recommendation you provide, they would be more likely to take action right away. We really look forward to reading your review.

Thanks again for your support and good luck!

If you enjoy my book, please write a POSITIVE REVIEW on amazon.

-- Dr. Peter Johnson --

Check Out Other Books

Go here to check out other related books that might interest you:

Legal Terminology And Phrases: Essential Legal Terms Explained You Need To Know About Crimes, Penalty And Criminal Procedure

http://www.amazon.com/dp/B01L5EB54Y

COMPANY LAW: Mastering Essential Legal Terms Explained About Limited Liability Companies, Joint-Stock Companies, Partnership, Private Enterprises, And Groups of Companies!

https://www.amazon.com/dp/B07P2PRVMJ

Legal Vocabulary In Use: Master 600+ Essential Legal Terms And Phrases Explained In 10 Minutes A Day

http://www.amazon.com/dp/B01L0FKXPU

Civil Law Vocabulary In Use: Master 350+ Essential Civil Law Terms And Phrases Explained With Examples In 10 Minutes A Day.

https://www.amazon.com/dp/B0781TQWGV

Criminal Law Vocabulary In Use: Master 400+ Essential Criminal Law Terms And Phrases Explained With Examples In 10 Minutes A Day.

https://www.amazon.com/dp/B078KLR51Z

Administrative And Tax Law In Use : Master 300+ Administrative And Tax Law Terms And Phrases Explained With Examples In 10 Minutes A Day.

https://www.amazon.com/dp/B07JMD546J

www.ingramcontent.com/pod-product-compliance
Lightning Source LLC
Chambersburg PA
CBHW030932060726
47591CB00005B/1762